L O U I S E   P

2004

A Book of Grace-Filled Days

LOYOLAPRESS.
CHICAGO

LOYOLAPRESS.
3441 N. ASHLAND AVENUE
CHICAGO, ILLINOIS 60657
(800) 621-1008
WWW.LOYOLABOOKS.ORG

Cover and interior design by Kathy Kikkert

Library of Congress Cataloging-in-Publication Data
Perrotta, Louise.
2004 : a book of grace-filled days / Louise Perrotta.
p. cm.
ISBN 0-8294-1455-X
1. Devotional calendars—Catholic Church. 2. Catholic Church—Prayer-books and devotions—English. I. Title.
BX2170.C56P47 2003
242'.3—dc21
2003000422

Printed in Canada

03 04 05 06 07 Webcom 10 9 8 7 6 5 4 3 2 1

INTRODUCTION

This book of brief lectionary-based meditations on Scripture is grounded in the premise that small things have power.

We're all familiar with this time-honored truth. We encounter it in the folk wisdom of proverbs like "An apple a day keeps the doctor away" and the nursery rhyme in which, "for want of a nail," everything "was lost"—from the horseshoe right through to the horse, rider, battle, war, and kingdom. We know the power of small things from countless experiences in everyday life. An aspirin brings relief. A crocus pushing up through the snow gives hope. A word of encouragement, a chance meeting, or a stray thought leads to some significant change. On the negative side are the effects of a virus, a hangnail, a loose wire, a termite, and a rumor.

In the Gospels, small things seem to get special attention. Jesus used many such images—a mustard seed, a buried grain of wheat, a talent on loan, a pearl, a cup of water given in his name, yeast, a speck in the eye—to illustrate their potential for good or ill. Using a boy's lunch, he provided food for thousands. He said that repentant tax collectors and prostitutes and other people considered small and lowly in the world would be revealed as gloriously exalted in the kingdom of heaven. Over and over, in many ways, Jesus drove the message home: If you want to be great, make yourself small (see Matthew 18:4).

But it's easy to nod agreement at the truth that small is powerful while neglecting it in practice. Small things are humble. They're easily missed, ignored, and underestimated. Saints like Thérèse of Lisieux didn't make this mistake. In fact, the "little way" to holiness that Thérèse lived and taught revolves around the loving fulfillment of all the small, ordinary tasks a person undertakes in living out his or her particular vocation.

2004: *A Book of Grace-Filled Days* is offered in the spirit of the "little way." Its goal is modest: to explore a small portion of Scripture by offering a brief meditation that connects it to simple events, thoughts, or daily-life encounters. Bible verses are taken from one of the readings of the day in the Roman Catholic lectionary. The full references for these readings are provided on each page.

Spending a few daily moments in reflection on God's word is a mustard-seed proposition with mustard-seed promise. After all, the Jesus who specializes in giving increase to small things is the one who invites you to meet him in his word. He offers you his Holy Spirit as a guide to understanding Scripture and how it connects with your life.

Come believing that Jesus wants to address you personally. Sit with him long enough to receive the graces he has for you each day. Over time, you will see your mustard-seed devotion grow into a plant large enough to provide both you and others with shelter in all of life's adversities (see Mark 4:31–32).

Sunday

NOVEMBER 30

• FIRST SUNDAY OF ADVENT •

For you I wait all the long day,
because of your goodness, LORD.
—PSALM 25:5

Not impatiently, as people do in checkout lines and traffic jams. Not fearfully, as if we were awaiting biopsy results or dental work. Not with an eye on the clock or the calendar, like bored and restive schoolkids.

No, Lord—this Advent, may we wait for you with joyful hope. Increase our eager longing as we pray, "Come, Lord Jesus!"

Jeremiah 33:14–16
Psalm 25
1 Thessalonians 3:12–4:2
Luke 21:25–28, 34–36

Monday

DECEMBER 1

The centurion said in reply, "Lord, I am not worthy to have you enter under my roof; only say the word and my servant will be healed. For I too am a person subject to authority, with soldiers subject to me. And I say to one, 'Go,' and he goes; and to another, 'Come here,' and he comes; and to my slave, 'Do this,' and he does it." When Jesus heard this, he was amazed.

—MATTHEW 8:8–10

The healing could take place whether or not Jesus was physically present: the centurion believed this with a faith that outshone even his striking humility and concern for his subordinate.

Anyone else who doesn't find the Lord physically present under his or her own roof can learn from the centurion and take heart.

Isaiah 2:1–5
Psalm 122
Matthew 8:5–11

Tuesday
DECEMBER 2

Turning to the disciples in private he said, "Blessed are the eyes that see what you see. For I say to you, many prophets and kings desired to see what you see, but did not see it, and to hear what you hear, but did not hear it."

—LUKE 10:23–24

It seemed to Brother Anthony that he had spent years looking at icons, holy cards, stained-glass windows, and statues of Jesus. But even after a lifetime of prayer, he knew he was only beginning to understand just who he was seeing.

Isaiah 11:1–10
Psalm 72
Luke 10:21–24

Wednesday

DECEMBER 3

• SAINT FRANCIS XAVIER, PRIEST •

On this mountain the LORD of hosts
will provide for all peoples
A feast of rich food and choice wines,
juicy, rich food and pure, choice wines.
—ISAIAH 25:6

When the prophets looked for a way to describe the indescribable—the condition of peace, justice, and life that characterizes God's kingdom—they often settled on the image of a lavish banquet.

This year, will my holiday feasting communicate anything of this prophetic image? Is there any little thing I could do to give the friends and family at my Christmas table a foretaste of the banquet of the kingdom?

Isaiah 25:6–10
Psalm 23
Matthew 15:29–37

Thursday

DECEMBER 4

• SAINT JOHN OF DAMASCUS, PRIEST AND DOCTOR OF THE CHURCH •

Better to take refuge in the LORD
than to put one's trust in mortals.
—PSALM 118:8

I ended the phone call feeling guilty. I had just done a hard sell on a woman who surely didn't have fifty extra dollars to pay for the towels I had talked her into buying. Just doing my job? In the catalog store where I worked, you were supposed to get customers to buy additional items after you took their phone orders. The more add-ons you brought in, the better your job prospects. Pressuring that woman to buy the towels was my "no more" moment. With all the trust I could muster, I put my job in the Lord's hands and asked him to show me a better way.

Isaiah 26:1–6
Psalm 118
Matthew 7:21, 24–27

Friday

DECEMBER 5

When he entered the house, the blind men approached him and Jesus said to them, "Do you believe that I can do this?" "Yes, Lord," they said to him. Then he touched their eyes and said, "Let it be done for you according to your faith." And their eyes were opened.

—MATTHEW 9:28–30

The two blind men had probably spent years begging at the gates in each other's company. Each one was intimately acquainted with the other's voice, smell, movements. But this was the first time they had ever looked at each other's faces.

In your life, are there other pairs of blind people who need that healing—that eye-opening kind of grace to look into a day-in, day-out companion's face and really see him or her for the first time? Where might that grace be waiting for you?

Isaiah 29:17–24
Psalm 27
Matthew 9:27–31

Saturday

DECEMBER 6

• SAINT NICHOLAS, BISHOP •

Jesus went around to all the towns and villages, teaching in their synagogues, proclaiming the gospel of the kingdom, and curing every disease and illness.

—MATTHEW 9:35

Traditions about St. Nicholas say he was a wonderworker who walked in Jesus' footsteps by healing the sick, helping the poor in miraculous ways, and even raising the dead.

People who reduce the saintly bishop to a Santa figure are settling for Christmas trinkets when they could be receiving the treasures of greater faith and openness to the miraculous ways in which God sometimes chooses to work.

Isaiah 30:19–21, 23–26
Psalm 147
Matthew 9:35–10:1, 5–8

Sunday

DECEMBER 7

• SECOND SUNDAY OF ADVENT •

Those who go forth weeping,
carrying sacks of seed,
Will return with cries of joy,
carrying their bundled sheaves.
—PSALM 126:6

Lugging heavy sheaves back from the field is ten times more arduous than carrying bags of seeds into it. It's not a vacation kind of joy that comes with a bountiful harvest, but the joy of successful hard work.

Baruch 5:1–9
Psalm 126
Philippians 1:4–6, 8–11
Luke 3:1–6

Monday

DECEMBER 8

• THE IMMACULATE CONCEPTION OF THE BLESSED VIRGIN MARY •

In him we were also chosen, destined in accord with the purpose of the One who accomplishes all things according to the intention of his will, so that we might exist for the praise of his glory, we who first hoped in Christ.

—EPHESIANS 1:11–12

The first person to be chosen in Christ was the first to demonstrate what it means to "exist for the praise of his glory."

Hail, Mary! You are the hope of all who hope in your Son.

Genesis 3:9–15, 20
Psalm 98
Ephesians 1:3–6, 11–12
Luke 1:26–38

Tuesday

DECEMBER 9

• SAINT JUAN DIEGO, HERMIT •

If a man has a hundred sheep and one of them goes astray, will he not leave the ninety-nine in the hills and go in search of the stray? And if he finds it, amen, I say to you, he rejoices more over it than over the ninety-nine that did not stray.

—MATTHEW 18:12–13

"Well, where *were* you?" ninety-nine annoyed sheep ask the rescued stray. "Out frolicking in greener pastures, we suppose. And meanwhile here we were, forced to eke out our dinner in a stubbly field with no shepherd. Who do you think you are, anyway?"

Enough taunting reproaches and any black sheep might be tempted to go astray again.

Isaiah 40:1–11
Psalm 96
Matthew 18:12–14

Wednesday

DECEMBER 10

Come to me, all you who labor and are burdened, and I will give you rest. Take my yoke upon you and learn from me, for I am meek and humble of heart; and you will find rest for yourselves. For my yoke is easy, and my burden light.

—MATTHEW 11:28–30

We know that you give us rest on Sunday, when we manage to take off the yoke of "business as usual." But you offer rest in the workweek too? A rest we can find even as we drop the kids off at childcare, sit in the marketing meeting, or try to calm a customer who's enraged because he was double-billed?

What is this rest, Lord? How can we experience it?

Isaiah 40:25–31
Psalm 103
Matthew 11:28–30

Thursday

DECEMBER 11

• SAINT DAMASUS I, POPE •

From the days of John the Baptist until now, the kingdom of heaven suffers violence, and the violent are taking it by force.
—MATTHEW 11:12

"You will become holy if you desire it," Blessed Marie of the Incarnation tells me. I get the feeling that she's not talking about an idle wish.

Get serious about prayer, St. Teresa of Ávila urges. Tell yourself, "I will keep going whether I reach the end of the journey or whether I die on the way."

While I don't know exactly what it means to take the kingdom of heaven by force, I do know that I admire the vigorous saints who pursued God with passion and energy.

Isaiah 41:13–20
Psalm 145
Matthew 11:11–15

Friday

DECEMBER 12

• OUR LADY OF GUADALUPE •

A great sign appeared in the sky, a woman clothed with the sun, with the moon under her feet, and on her head a crown of twelve stars.

—REVELATION 12:1

When the people of Nazareth looked at Mary, they saw a young mother who made hummus, chatted with neighbors, and drew water at the well, like all the other village women. What God saw was a woman clothed with the sun and crowned with stars.

What if God's hidden grace in people's lives were suddenly unveiled? What would we see in that elderly couple at church, in that squirming toddler—even in that fourteen year old who always gives herself a manicure during the homily?

Zechariah 2:14–17 or Revelation 11:19; 12:1–6, 10
Psalm 45
Luke 1:26–38 or Luke 1:39–47 or any readings from the Common of the Blessed Virgin Mary, nos. 707–712

Saturday

DECEMBER 13

• SAINT LUCY, VIRGIN AND MARTYR •

By God's word he shut up the heavens
and three times brought down fire.
How awesome are you, ELIJAH!
Whose glory is equal to yours?
—SIRACH 48:3–4

The rhetorical question refers to human beings only. The biblical author would never have put miracle-working Elijah on the same plane as the incomparably glorious God who makes the miracles possible.

Do I have the same clarity about devotions, indulgences, and the saints' intercession? Am I putting my faith in the God who works miracles or in persons and things that are said to "always work"?

Sirach 48:1–4, 9–11
Psalm 80
Matthew 17:9–13

Sunday

DECEMBER 14

• THIRD SUNDAY OF ADVENT •

Even tax collectors came to be baptized and they said to him, "Teacher, what should we do?" He answered them, "Stop collecting more than what is prescribed." Soldiers also asked him, "And what is it that we should do?" He told them, "Do not practice extortion, do not falsely accuse anyone, and be satisfied with your wages."

—LUKE 3:12–14

Paul and Erica decided not to live together before they got married, unlike all their friends. Jim said no to the shady and lucrative deal that his business friends came up with. Melissa got flak from other kids for refusing to cheat on tests.

When you're faced with "everybody's doing it" situations, just sticking to the basic moral norm can be an act of heroic virtue.

Zephaniah 3:14–18
Isaiah 12:2–6
Philippians 4:4–7
Luke 3:10–18

Monday

DECEMBER 15

I see him, though not now;
I behold him, though not near:
A star shall advance from Jacob,
and a staff shall rise from Israel.
—NUMBERS 24:17

We journey toward the Lord, as the Magi did two millennia ago. Without knowing him, they sought him, their eyes scanning the horizon for the rising star that would fill their hearts with joy.

We know the one we seek. Why don't we stay on course, then, and keep traveling on, even when our horizons seem to stretch out bleak and starless?

Brother Magi, fellow travelers, pray for us.

Numbers 24:2–7, 15–17
Psalm 25
Matthew 21:23–27

Tuesday

DECEMBER 16

What is your opinion?

—MATTHEW 21:28

Even when he was dealing with people he knew were hostile to him, Jesus took the risk of appealing to their goodwill, sense of fairness, and ability to reason out the right conclusion.

Jesus, help me become more willing to take that risk too.

Zephaniah 3:1–2, 9–13
Psalm 34
Matthew 21:28–32

Wednesday

DECEMBER 17

Abiud became the father of Eliakim, Eliakim the father of Azor, Azor the father of Zadok. Zadok became the father of Achim, Achim the father of Eliud, Eliud the father of Eleazar. Eleazar became the father of Matthan, Matthan the father of Jacob, Jacob the father of Joseph, the husband of Mary.

—MATTHEW 1:13–16

Whenever you're feeling like an unimportant nobody with little influence and little chance of making a mark in the world, take a look at Jesus' family tree. Nothing is known about some of these ancestors, yet even the most obscure among them played a role in history's most important event.

Genesis 49:2, 8–10
Psalm 72
Matthew 1:1–17

Thursday

DECEMBER 18

Therefore, the days will come, says the LORD, when they shall no longer say, "As the LORD lives, who brought the Israelites out of the land of Egypt"; but rather, "As the LORD lives, who brought the descendants of the house of Israel up from the land of the north."

—JEREMIAH 23:7–8

Remembering God's mighty deeds in the past fuels our faith that God will work mighty deeds in the future. Whenever we forget, our life in the present turns to wistful nostalgia.

Jeremiah 23:5–8
Psalm 72
Matthew 1:18–25

Friday

DECEMBER 19

But now you will be speechless and unable to talk until the day these things take place, because you did not believe my words, which will be fulfilled at their proper time.

—LUKE 1:20

Zechariah's muteness was a punishment for doubting the birth announcement brought to him by the angel Gabriel, but it was also a confirming sign that this joyful and amazing event would indeed come to pass. Zechariah's nine-month retreat was silent, but not somber.

Judges 13:2–7, 24–25
Psalm 71
Luke 1:5–25

Saturday

DECEMBER 20

Again the LORD spoke to Ahaz: Ask for a sign from the LORD, your God; let it be deep as the nether world, or high as the sky! But Ahaz answered, "I will not ask! I will not tempt the LORD!"

—ISAIAH 7:10–12

Today, Lord, I will not shrug off your invitations to deeper faith. With your help, I will shed the fear and apathy and false humility that keep me from accepting them.

Isaiah 7:10–14
Psalm 24
Luke 1:26–38

Sunday

DECEMBER 21

• FOURTH SUNDAY OF ADVENT •

For at the moment the sound of your greeting reached my ears, the infant in my womb leaped for joy.

—LUKE 1:44

We recognize those who bear your life within them by the way they cause our spirits to quicken and our hearts to leap with glad hope in you. Through their words, your Word is born in us.

Micah 5:1–4
Psalm 80
Hebrews 10:5–10
Luke 1:39–45

Monday

DECEMBER 22

Once [Samuel] was weaned, [Hannah] . . . presented him at the temple of the LORD. . . . "I prayed for this child, and the LORD granted my request. Now I, in turn, give him to the LORD; as long as he lives, he shall be dedicated to the LORD." She left him there.

—1 SAMUEL 1:24, 27–28

While St. Monica shows us how to pray for our children when they are lost, Hannah shows us how to surrender them. As we wave goodbye at the school-bus stop, wait by a sickbed, or walk a daughter down the aisle, we can reflect on Hannah's example of how to relinquish our children with trust into the hands of the One who entrusted them to us.

1 Samuel 1:24–28
1 Samuel 2:1, 4–8
Luke 1:46–56

Tuesday

DECEMBER 23

• SAINT JOHN OF KANTY, PRIEST •

When they came on the eighth day to circumcise the child, they were going to call him Zechariah after his father, but his mother said in reply, "No. He will be called John." But they answered her, "There is no one among your relatives who has this name." So they made signs, asking his father what he wished him to be called. He asked for a tablet and wrote, "John is his name."

—LUKE 1:59–63

Where in your life is God calling you to something new? What sign will you use to declare your intent to follow the Spirit's leading?

Malachi 3:1–4, 23–24
Psalm 25
Luke 1:57–66

Wednesday

DECEMBER 24

. . . the tender mercy of our God
by which the daybreak from on high will visit us
to shine on those who sit in darkness and death's shadow,
to guide our feet into the path of peace.
—LUKE 1:78–79

Because the rising of the sun is an image of Christ's coming into a dark world, early Christians prayed facing east and oriented their churches in that direction. It feels natural to do the same today, especially for morning prayer. The real issue, though, is whether I go on to live the rest of my day in an east-facing direction. Is my whole life catching the transforming rays of "the daybreak from on high"?

2 Samuel 7:1–5, 8–12, 14, 16
Psalm 89
Luke 1:67–79

Thursday

DECEMBER 25

• THE NATIVITY OF THE LORD • CHRISTMAS •

While they were there, the time came for her to have her child, and she gave birth to her firstborn son. She wrapped him in swaddling clothes and laid him in a manger, because there was no room for them in the inn.

—LUKE 2:6–7

You created the universe, split the sea, revealed your majesty in pillars of fire and in mountains that quaked. We know you are a God of glory, Lord. But it takes this Child, lying in a manger, to show us that you are also little.

Vigil:
Isaiah 62:1–5
Psalm 89
Acts 13:16–17, 22–25
Matthew 1:1–25 or 1:18–25

Midnight:
Isaiah 9:1–6
Psalm 96
Titus 2:11–14
Luke 2:1–14

Dawn:
Isaiah 62:11–12
Psalm 97
Titus 3:4–7
Luke 2:15–20

Day:
Isaiah 52:7–10
Psalm 98
Hebrews 1:1–6
John 1:1–18 or 1:1–5, 9–14

Friday

DECEMBER 26

• SAINT STEPHEN, FIRST MARTYR •

When they hand you over, do not worry about how you are to speak or what you are to say. You will be given at that moment what you are to say. For it will not be you who speak but the Spirit of your Father speaking through you.

—MATTHEW 10:19–20

What kind of person derives comfort from this reassurance of God's presence during persecution? Only the kind who gives higher priority to faithfully communicating the gospel and bearing witness to Christ than to staying alive.

Acts 6:8–10; 7:54–59
Psalm 31
Matthew 10:17–22

Saturday

DECEMBER 27

• SAINT JOHN, APOSTLE AND EVANGELIST •

[Simon Peter] went into the tomb and saw the burial cloths there, and the cloth that had covered his head, not with the burial cloths but rolled up in a separate place. Then the other disciple also went in, the one who had arrived at the tomb first, and he saw and believed.

—JOHN 20:6–8

My living-room floor is decorated with ribbon bits and scattered wads of gift-wrap. It doesn't take a detective to figure out what happened here two days ago. Just read the evidence.

That's what the apostle John did. Struck by something unusual about Jesus' burial cloths, he interpreted the clues and was instantly convinced. We're like John: we don't see Jesus, but we do see signs that point us toward the truth. Do we read the evidence and profess that he is truly risen?

1 John 1:1–4
Psalm 97
John 20:1–8

Sunday

DECEMBER 28

• THE HOLY FAMILY OF JESUS, MARY, AND JOSEPH •

How lovely your dwelling,
O LORD of hosts! . . .
Happy are those who dwell in your house!
They never cease to praise you.
—PSALM 84:2, 5

Joseph built a house for his family. Mary made it a home. Jesus prepared a place for them in his Father's house, where they now live in glory—and in joyful expectation that, before too long, its many dwelling places will be occupied by the other members of the family.

Sirach 3:2–7, 12–14 or 1 Samuel 1:20–22, 24–28
Psalm 128 or Psalm 84
Colossians 3:12–21 or 3:12–17 or 1 John 3:1–2, 21–24
Luke 2:41–52

Monday

DECEMBER 29

• SAINT THOMAS BECKET, BISHOP AND MARTYR •

[T]he holy Spirit was upon him. It had been revealed to him by the holy Spirit that he should not see death before he had seen the Messiah of the Lord. He came in the Spirit into the temple.

—LUKE 2:25–27

When you live in the company of the Holy Spirit, your spiritual vision gets keener, even as your eyesight fails, and you stand a better chance of being where the action is than do those younger, driven types who rarely find the time to listen.

1 John 2:3–11
Psalm 96
Luke 2:22–35

Tuesday

DECEMBER 30

There was also a prophetess, Anna, the daughter of Phanuel, of the tribe of Asher. She was advanced in years, having lived seven years with her husband after her marriage, and then as a widow until she was eighty-four. She never left the temple, but worshiped night and day with fasting and prayer.

—LUKE 2:36–37

Meredith was irritated by the elderly women in the weekday Mass crowd. *So nosy,* she thought when they greeted her. "So noisy," she pronounced when they prayed the rosary out loud. "So out of it," she sniffed dismissively.

When her father died, though, these were the parishioners who reached out to Meredith—with holy cards, comforting words, homemade pies. "So wise, so kind," Meredith reflected. "I hope I'm like them someday."

1 John 2:12–17
Psalm 96
Luke 2:36–40

Wednesday

DECEMBER 31

• SAINT SYLVESTER I, POPE • NEW YEAR'S EVE •

And the Word became flesh
and made his dwelling among us,
and we saw his glory.
—JOHN 1:14

"Teacher, where are you staying?" Andrew and John asked you.
"Come, and you will see," you said (John 1:38–39).
We're coming too, Lord. We want to see.

You dwell among us—this we know.
But how often, in the past twelve months, we passed you by without a second glance.
Lead us to the places where you dwell.
Let us see your glory and recognize you, O Living Word, in the coming year's encounters and events.

1 John 2:18–21
Psalm 96
John 1:1–18

Thursday

JANUARY 1

• THE BLESSED VIRGIN MARY, MOTHER OF GOD • NEW YEAR'S DAY •

The LORD bless you and keep you!
The LORD let his face shine upon you,
and be gracious to you!
The LORD look upon you kindly and give you peace!
—NUMBERS 6:24–26

On this day, when my father was alive, I used to phone home to ask him for his blessing. It's an old French-Canadian custom I inherited. Very simply, speaking from the heart, Dad would ask the Lord to keep me in his care in the coming year.

I still ask my father for his yearly blessing—though not by phone. And I receive it joyfully, as a joint gift from him and from the Father who is the source of every blessing.

Numbers 6:22–27
Psalm 67
Galatians 4:4–7
Luke 2:16–21

Friday

JANUARY 2

• SAINTS BASIL THE GREAT AND GREGORY NAZIANZEN, BISHOPS AND DOCTORS OF THE CHURCH •

So they said to him, "Who are you, so we can give an answer to those who sent us?"

—JOHN 1:22

Then the rugged man in the camelhair clothing squared his shoulders, pushed out his chest, and made it clear that, as the chief emissary of history's most important VIP, he should be approached with the deference befitting his status . . .

Just kidding. Could John the Baptist possibly have taken a more radically *un*selfimportant approach?: "I am 'the voice of one crying out in the desert, "Make straight the way of the Lord"'" (John 1:23).

1 John 2:22–28
Psalm 98
John 1:19–28

Saturday

JANUARY 3

The next day he saw Jesus coming toward him and said, "Behold, the Lamb of God, who takes away the sin of the world."

—JOHN 1:29

John the Baptist recognized the Lamb of God in the dusty figure who approached him on the banks of the Jordan River. At every Mass, we recognize him under the appearances too.

1 John 2:29–3:6
Psalm 98
John 1:29–34

Sunday

JANUARY 4

• THE EPIPHANY OF THE LORD •

They were overjoyed at seeing the star, and on entering the house they saw the child with Mary his mother. They prostrated themselves and did him homage. Then they opened their treasures and offered him gifts of gold, frankincense, and myrrh.

—MATTHEW 2:10–11

How is it that after traveling so far, through so many dangers and at such great cost, the wise men felt more than amply repaid for their trouble by the ordinary domestic scene they found at journey's end?

How is it that today's armchair traveler can follow in their footsteps and experience the same joy of discovery?

Isaiah 60:1–6
Psalm 72
Ephesians 3:2–3, 5–6
Matthew 2:1–12

Monday

JANUARY 5

• SAINT JOHN NEUMANN, BISHOP •

Beloved, do not trust every spirit but test the spirits to see whether they belong to God.

—1 JOHN 4:1

Since he lived in a university town that was awash in spirituality, Eddie seized the opportunity to participate in various small-group explorations. Soul travel, tarot, shamanic journeying, astrology, runic meditation, Sufi dancing, numerology, anthroposophy, modern druidry—Eddie was enthused about them all.

He did wonder, though, as he joined his latest spirituality circle in outdoor chanting to the star goddess, how a person could really know whether any of it was true.

1 John 3:22–4:6
Psalm 2
Matthew 4:12–17, 23–25

Tuesday

JANUARY 6

• BLESSED ANDRÉ BESSETTE, RELIGIOUS •

He asked them, "How many loaves do you have? . . . " [T]hey said, "Five loaves and two fish."

—MARK 6:38

More than five thousand hungry mouths to feed, and just a few mouthfuls of food with which to do it. Why bother?

We all face "why bother?" situations, where our resources look hopelessly insufficient compared to the needs. But unless we give the little we can scrape up, what will Jesus have to work with? Why bother giving our snack? Because if we don't, people will go hungry, and we'll never see that snack multiplied into a banquet with twelve baskets of leftovers.

1 John 4:7–10
Psalm 72
Mark 6:34–44

Wednesday

JANUARY 7

• SAINT RAYMOND OF PEÑAFORT, PRIEST •

Then he saw that they were tossed about while rowing, for the wind was against them. About the fourth watch of the night, he came towards them walking on the sea. He meant to pass by them.

—MARK 6:48

Did Jesus really intend to "pass by" the disciples in their distress? Was it some kind of a test? I'm more persuaded by another possibility—that Jesus' passing by was meant to evoke the experiences of Moses and Elijah, who watched as God revealed himself by "passing by" in beauty and glory (Exodus 33:19, 22; 1 Kings 19:11).

Lord Jesus, how are you passing by your disciples today?

1 John 4:11–18
Psalm 72
Mark 6:45–52

Thursday

JANUARY 8

If anyone says, "I love God," but hates his brother, he is a liar; for whoever does not love a brother whom he has seen cannot love God whom he has not seen.

—1 JOHN 4:20

Adriana had great admiration for the saints, but reading their lives always made her feel condemned. "Do I love God, compared to them? Not much," she'd sigh hopelessly. She shelved her aspirations for spiritual improvement until, one day, she glimpsed a way to make a tiny bit of progress: "I'll be kinder to Michelle. I think I can manage that." Maybe this approach would help her get her foot in the door to greater love of God.

1 John 4:19–5:4
Psalm 72
Luke 4:14–22

Friday

JANUARY 9

The report about him spread all the more, and great crowds assembled to listen to him and to be cured of their ailments, but he would withdraw to deserted places to pray.

—LUKE 5:15–16

My five-year-old computer is so overloaded with software that it moves very slowly and crashes twice a day. I'm like that too when I'm overloaded, until I click on my "restart" button—prayer.

1 John 5:5–13
Psalm 147
Luke 5:12–16

Saturday

JANUARY 10

Let them praise his name in festive dance,
make music with tambourine and lyre. . . .
[C]ry out for joy at their banquet,
With the praise of God in their mouths.

—PSALM 149:3, 5–6

Ho hum. We'll have the opening prayers and then the readings, the ho-hum homily and the ho-hum response. Then it will be over, and we'll get in our cars and drive home.

With so many more reasons for praising God than the psalmists ever dreamed possible, why the ho hum? Maybe if we thought more about what it is we celebrate at every eucharistic banquet, we'd feel more like getting out the cymbals too!

1 John 5:14–21
Psalm 149
John 3:22–30

Sunday

JANUARY 11

• THE BAPTISM OF THE LORD •

For the grace of God has appeared, saving all and training us to reject godless ways and worldly desires and to live temperately, justly, and devoutly in this age.

—TITUS 2:11–12

The grace of God is like a personal trainer who assesses the condition of your body, tests your muscle tone, estimates your potential, and designs a bodybuilding workout tailored to your needs.

Jesus, you know better than anyone how much I need a customized training program for the soul! Will you be my personal trainer? I promise to accept every grueling workout as a grace.

Isaiah 42:1–4, 6–7 or Isaiah 40:1–5, 9–11
Psalm 29
Acts 10:34–38 or Titus 2:11–14; 3:4–7
Luke 3:15–16, 21–22

Monday

JANUARY 12

So they left their father Zebedee in the boat along with the hired men and followed him.

—MARK 1:20

Zebedee was a respectable businessman and head of household. Did he wonder why Jesus didn't recruit him too? When his own call to discipleship came, did he hear it?

"Why is my life different from that person's?" "Why haven't I received the same grace as my friend?" Who can say? God has six billion different ways of calling six billion different people. If we resist envy at how grace comes to others, we're less likely to miss the boat when grace comes to us.

1 Samuel 1:1–8
Psalm 116
Mark 1:14–20

Tuesday

JANUARY 13

• SAINT HILARY, BISHOP AND DOCTOR OF THE CHURCH •

His fame spread everywhere throughout the whole region of Galilee.
—MARK 1:28

"The way he teaches, I figure he's a superscribe," said one man after hearing Jesus. "No, he's mainly a healer," said another. "Didn't you see how he cured that little kid?" A third person gestured impatiently. "You two are so stupid. He's a revolutionary, obviously, the one who's going to rid us of these Romans!"

However we try to peg Jesus, he's always much more than we think. The "unclean spirit" got it right: "I know who you are—the Holy One of God!" (Mark 1:24).

1 Samuel 1:9–20
1 Samuel 2:1, 4–8
Mark 1:21–28

Wednesday

JANUARY 14

Speak, for your servant is listening.

—1 SAMUEL 3:10

The heavens declare your glory. The stones cry out. Mountains and hills rejoice. Praise wells up from the mouths of infants. Your people tell your mighty deeds. Your word is at work among us. The signs of the times speak of you.

You have so many ways of speaking to your servants, Lord! Give us ears attuned to your communications.

1 Samuel 3:1–10, 19–20

Psalm 40

Mark 1:29–39

Thursday

JANUARY 15

When the troops retired to the camp, the elders of Israel said, "Why has the LORD permitted us to be defeated today by the Philistines? Let us fetch the ark of the LORD from Shiloh that it may go into battle among us and save us from the grasp of our enemies."

—1 SAMUEL 4:3

If you really want to know where you went wrong, get the answer to your question before plunging ahead again. Unless you stop and listen, you'll repeat the same mistake in different ways, with more disastrous consequences.

1 Samuel 4:1–11
Psalm 44
Mark 1:40–45

Friday

JANUARY 16

The people, however, refused to listen to Samuel's warning and said, "Not so! There must be a king over us. We too must be like other nations, with a king to rule us and to lead us in warfare and fight our battles." When Samuel had listened to all the people had to say, he repeated it to the LORD, who then said to him, "Grant their request and appoint a king to rule them."

—1 SAMUEL 8:19–22

Tony had always been basically serious about following the Lord. Even so, how many detours he had unwittingly taken in his life! Now, on the eve of his ordination to the priesthood, he understood more clearly that a merciful God had worked with him all the way, accommodating his plans to each of Tony's wrong turns and steering him back on course.

1 Samuel 8:4–7, 10–22
Psalm 89
Mark 2:1–12

Saturday

JANUARY 17

• SAINT ANTHONY, ABBOT •

Those who are well do not need a physician, but the sick do.

—MARK 2:17

But in this case, the healing they need comes from a personal relationship with the doctor. The medicine is the Physician.

1 Samuel 9:1–4, 17–19; 10:1
Psalm 21
Mark 2:13–17

Sunday

JANUARY 18

When the wine ran short, the mother of Jesus said to him, "They have no wine." . . . His mother said to the servers, "Do whatever he tells you."

—JOHN 2:3, 5

We all know people who have a gift for helping others make beneficial connections. They're the networkers who are generous with their insights and resources. They're the ones who know exactly who should sit together at dinner parties, the ones who tell us, "Jim's just the person you should meet." Often in humble, hidden ways, they fill the gap between our need and its fulfillment.

Jesus' mother was like that. She still is.

Isaiah 62:1–5
Psalm 96
1 Corinthians 12:4–11
John 2:1–11

Monday

JANUARY 19

• MARTIN LUTHER KING JR. DAY •

No one sews a piece of unshrunken cloth on an old cloak. If he does, its fullness pulls away, the new from the old, and the tear gets worse. Likewise, no one pours new wine into old wineskins. Otherwise, the wine will burst the skins, and both the wine and the skins are ruined. Rather, new wine is poured into fresh wineskins.

—MARK 2:21–22

At work, Peter was valued for his innovative ideas, his ability to "think outside the box" in response to changing needs and opportunities. It took a long time before he realized that he needed a similar approach in his thinking about God, which he had kept confined to the same little mental box he had been carrying around since first-communion class.

1 Samuel 15:16–23
Psalm 50
Mark 2:18–22

Tuesday

JANUARY 20

• SAINT FABIAN, POPE AND MARTYR • SAINT SEBASTIAN, MARTYR •

Not as man sees does God see, because man sees the appearance but the LORD *looks into the heart.*

—1 SAMUEL 16:7

Three months ago, a fast-food worker charged me a quarter for coffee: it was my first senior-citizen discount. *What is she thinking?* I thought sullenly as I paid up.

Three weeks ago, a supermarket clerk ran my lettuce, blueberries, and six-pack of beer through the scanner, then asked to verify my ID. *What is she thinking?* I wondered, glowing and fishing in my bag for my driver's license.

But what am *I* thinking if I'm more concerned with what my outer appearance says to others than with what my inner appearance says to God?

1 Samuel 16:1–13
Psalm 89
Mark 2:23–28

Wednesday

JANUARY 21

• SAINT AGNES, VIRGIN AND MARTYR •

Then he said to them, "Is it lawful to do good on the sabbath rather than to do evil, to save life rather than to destroy it?" But they remained silent. Looking around at them with anger and grieved at their hardness of heart, he said to the man, "Stretch out your hand."

—MARK 3:4–5

The hardheartedness that withers the soul is more devastating than the wasting disease that shrivels the limb. When we encounter it within ourselves, Jesus' kind of anger is the only appropriate response.

1 Samuel 17:32–33, 37, 40–51
Psalm 144
Mark 3:1–6

Thursday

JANUARY 22

• SAINT VINCENT, DEACON AND MARTYR •

My wanderings you have noted;
are my tears not stored in your vial,
recorded in your book?
—PSALM 56:9

While watching at a saintly nun's deathbed, St. Thérèse of Lisieux caught the woman's last tear on a handkerchief. She treasured the keepsake to the end of her life.

How much more precious our tears are to the Lord, who will one day "wipe away the tears from all faces" (Isaiah 25:8).

1 Samuel 18:6–9; 19:1–7
Psalm 56
Mark 3:7–12

Friday

JANUARY 23

May God send help from heaven to save me,
shame those who trample upon me.
—PSALM 57:4

When my sins weigh me down and smother me,
shame them into submission, Lord!

When the enemy who kills the soul prowls about me like a hungry lion,
crush him underfoot!

When other people treat me unkindly,
show them your love
so that they will be ashamed of their ways.
May they trample their own hardheartedness
and imitate your mercy.

1 Samuel 24:3–21
Psalm 57
Mark 3:13–19

Saturday

JANUARY 24

• SAINT FRANCIS DE SALES, BISHOP AND DOCTOR OF THE CHURCH •

[Jesus] came home. Again [the] crowd gathered, making it impossible for them even to eat. When his relatives heard of this they set out to seize him, for they said, "He is out of his mind."

—MARK 3:20–21

Jesus' relatives decided it was time for a family intervention.

Before passing judgment on them, perhaps I should remind myself of the times when my own concern for a family member led me to some well-intentioned but misguided take-charge action.

Lord, give us the wisdom to detect your activity in other people's lives so that we won't step in and squelch it.

2 Samuel 1:1–4, 11–12, 19, 23–27
Psalm 80
Mark 3:20–21

Sunday

JANUARY 25

Ezra read plainly from the book of the law of God, interpreting it so that all could understand what was read. . . . [A]ll the people were weeping as they heard the words of the law.

—NEHEMIAH 8:8–9

Ezra was a Jewish priest addressing a Jerusalem congregation of returned exiles. His "interpretation" was probably translation: during their sojourn in Aramaic-speaking Babylonia, most of the exiles had forgotten their Hebrew, the language of the "book of the law of God."

Today, as I listen to God's word proclaimed at Mass, I will not need a translator. But what will it take for me to allow these familiar words to cut me to the heart?

Nehemiah 8:2–6, 8–10
Psalm 19
1 Corinthians 12:12–30 or 12:12–14, 27
Luke 1:1–4; 4:14–21

Monday

JANUARY 26

• SAINTS TIMOTHY AND TITUS, BISHOPS •

For this reason I left you in Crete so that you might set right what remains to be done and appoint presbyters in every town, as I directed you.

—TITUS 1:5

We're jogging along the pathway by the river. My heart pounding, my muscles aching, I gasp for enough air to ask a question: "Tell me again, now: why are we doing this?" And my husband, who is always good for an explanation, obligingly speaks of muscle tone, bone density, the value of aerobic exercise, and the joys of being outdoors.

When your energy is flagging and once-clear goals have gotten hazy, there's nothing like a timely reminder to get you back on track.

2 Timothy 1:1–8 or Titus 1:1–5
Psalm 37
Mark 3:22–30

Tuesday

JANUARY 27

• SAINT ANGELA MERICI, VIRGIN •

Then David, girt with a linen apron, came dancing before the LORD with abandon, as he and all the Israelites were bringing up the ark of the LORD with shouts of joy and to the sound of the horn.

—2 SAMUEL 6:14–15

David put on his apron—a priestly garment worn for liturgical celebrations—and fixed his whole attention on rejoicing in the Lord. How often do I take off my apron—my anxious workday thoughts and cares—so as to do the same?

2 Samuel 6:12–15, 17–19
Psalm 24
Mark 3:31–35

Wednesday

JANUARY 28

• SAINT THOMAS AQUINAS, PRIEST AND DOCTOR OF THE CHURCH •

And some seed fell on rich soil and produced fruit. It came up and grew and yielded thirty, sixty, and a hundredfold.

—MARK 4:8

Once, in a public debate about religion, an atheist challenged a Catholic university student, "What do *you* do besides talk to prove the faith you claim is in you?"

The challenge made the student realize that he was mostly a hearer of the word, not a doer. He began visiting the sick and helping the needy. It was the beginning of the St. Vincent de Paul Society, whose worldwide ministry continues today—all because Frédéric Ozanam recognized and welcomed God's word when it came to him.

2 Samuel 7:4–17
Psalm 89
Mark 4:1–20

Thursday

JANUARY 29

For there is nothing hidden except to be made visible; nothing is secret except to come to light.

—MARK 4:22

Which hidden things? Which secrets? When Jesus comes again, will he take our lifetime's worth of covert sins and weaknesses and project them on a skywide screen for all the world to see? Or will the main feature be a showing that unveils mysteries of God's kingdom—for those with eyes to see?

2 Samuel 7:18–19, 24–29
Psalm 132
Mark 4:21–25

Friday

JANUARY 30

The next morning David wrote a letter to Joab which he sent by Uriah. In it he directed: "Place Uriah up front, where the fighting is fierce. Then pull back and leave him to be struck down dead."

—2 SAMUEL 11:14–15

The Bible's authors and editors didn't omit the warts and blemishes from the portraits they presented—not even when the result put important characters like David in a very bad light.

When I come before God, do I take the same honest approach to my own sins and weaknesses, or do I get out the airbrush?

2 Samuel 11:1–10, 13–17
Psalm 51
Mark 4:26–34

Saturday

JANUARY 31

• SAINT JOHN BOSCO, PRIEST •

Do you not yet have faith?

—MARK 4:40

Tonight I will set my alarm and trust it to rouse me at the right time. Tomorrow morning I will shower, eat my toast, and drive to the post office—thereby expressing my faith in the plumber, the electrician, the grocer, the farmer, the car mechanic, road crews, numerous other drivers, and countless postal workers. I will talk to relatives, friends, neighbors, and colleagues without once feeling that I can't believe a word they say.

Why, you'd think that a person who is so inclined to trust would feel absolutely no resistance to putting her faith in God!

2 Samuel 12:1–7, 10–17
Psalm 51
Mark 4:35–41

Sunday

FEBRUARY 1

If I speak in human and angelic tongues but do not have love, I am a resounding gong or a clashing cymbal.

—1 CORINTHIANS 13:1

So opens the biblical passage that is often considered the most beautiful praise of love ever penned. But how annoyed its author would be if anyone tried to give him an award in the "most inspirational" category! Paul shied away from what he called "sublimity of words" (1 Corinthians 2:1). He put the priority on loving action.

What about us? If we're more inclined to send a greeting card than to perform a loving service, it's time to reassess.

Jeremiah 1:4–5, 17–19
Psalm 71
1 Corinthians 12:31–13:13 or 13:4–13
Luke 4:21–30

Monday

FEBRUARY 2

• THE PRESENTATION OF THE LORD •

Lift up your heads, O gates;
rise up, you ancient portals,
that the king of glory may enter.
—PSALM 24:7

The Sahara is expanding, flowing into some West Central African villages at such a rate that people have to dig out their doorways every morning.

Though I'm not threatened by desert sands, I need to dig out regularly too. The doorway of my heart gets silted up so quickly! Unless I do some regular excavating with my prayer shovel, how will the King of glory enter?

Malachi 3:1–4
Psalm 24
Hebrews 2:14–18
Luke 2:22–40 or 2:22–32

Tuesday

FEBRUARY 3

• SAINT BLAISE, BISHOP AND MARTYR • SAINT ANSGAR, BISHOP •

The king was shaken, and went up to the room over the city gate to weep. He said as he wept, "My son Absalom! My son, my son Absalom! If only I had died instead of you, Absalom, my son, my son!"

—2 SAMUEL 19:1

The great mystery of our faith is that we have a Father who lovingly chose to exchange his life for ours and who found a way to do so through his Son.

2 Samuel 18:9–10, 14, 24–25, 30–19:3
Psalm 86
Mark 5:21–43

Wednesday

FEBRUARY 4

[H]e began to teach in the synagogue, and many who heard him were astonished. They said, "Where did this man get all this? What kind of wisdom has been given him? What mighty deeds are wrought by his hands! Is he not the carpenter . . . ?" And they took offense at him.

—MARK 6:2–3

After many years away, I've returned to the city where I used to live. Things have changed. My friends' sons and daughters are coming into their own. John speaks Mandarin. Cait gives savvy legal advice. Andrew is my computer guru. Where did they get all this? How did it happen? Where are the children whose noses I used to wipe?

Only by reassessing my relationships with them will I open myself to the new possibilities of friendship and expertise that they offer.

2 Samuel 24:2, 9–17
Psalm 32
Mark 6:1–6

Thursday

FEBRUARY 5

• SAINT AGATHA, VIRGIN AND MARTYR •

Riches and honor are from you,
and you have dominion over all.
In your hand are power and might;
it is yours to give grandeur and strength to all.
—1 CHRONICLES 29:12

So I'm asking you real nice, dear God, please give me all these things. I'll use them only for good, as your faithful steward. I'll help people—really I will. You know I'm not the type to let money and power go to my head. So how about it, Lord?

Did St. Agatha pray like this, I wonder? Did any saint?

1 Kings 2:1–4, 10–12
1 Chronicles 29:10–12
Mark 6:7–13

Friday

FEBRUARY 6

• SAINT PAUL MIKI AND HIS COMPANIONS, MARTYRS •

Herod feared John, knowing him to be a righteous and holy man, and kept him in custody. When he heard him speak he was very much perplexed, yet he liked to listen to him.

—MARK 6:20

Who was the real prisoner? The one who wore the chains or the one who was too bound by indecision and public opinion to change the way he lived?

Sirach 47:2–11
Psalm 18
Mark 6:14–29

Saturday

FEBRUARY 7

He said to them, "Come away by yourselves to a deserted place and rest a while." People were coming and going in great numbers, and they had no opportunity even to eat. So they went off in the boat by themselves to a deserted place. People saw them leaving and many came to know about it. They hastened there on foot from all the towns and arrived at the place before them.

—MARK 6:31–33

Even when the press of demands and duties leaves you just a few minutes' time alone in the boat with Jesus, it's always worth accepting his invitation to climb aboard.

1 Kings 3:4–13
Psalm 119
Mark 6:30–34

Sunday

FEBRUARY 8

Getting into one of the boats, the one belonging to Simon, he asked him to put out a short distance from the shore.

—LUKE 5:3

"I'm exhausted," Simon could have answered Jesus. "Can't you get Jacob over there to take you in his boat? He hasn't been fishing all night." Then, of course, he would have missed the opportunity to "put out into deep water" (Luke 5:4) for that net-breaking catch.

Jesus, make me alert to the opportunities you send my way today.

Isaiah 6:1–8
Psalm 138
1 Corinthians 15:1–11 or 15:3–8, 11
Luke 5:1–11

Monday

FEBRUARY 9

Your priests will be clothed with justice;
your faithful will shout for joy.
—PSALM 132:9

No one who attends the heavenly banquet will have to agonize over what to wear. The host himself will provide the festal garments—the "robe of salvation" and "mantle of justice" (Isaiah 61:10)—and will work the internal change they signify.

Gathered together as God's whole people, we will rejoice heartily in the Lord, who has made us good and just, from the inside out.

1 Kings 8:1–7, 9–13
Psalm 132
Mark 6:53–56

Tuesday

FEBRUARY 10

• SAINT SCHOLASTICA, VIRGIN •

He went on to say, "How well you have set aside the commandment of God in order to uphold your tradition!"

—MARK 7:9

Emily had a vague recollection that a saint had once told someone it was all right to leave off praying in order to answer a request for help—something about leaving Christ in prayer to find him in service to others. That became her excuse for skipping prayer whenever it felt difficult. And whenever she encountered an inconvenient request for help, she begged off by remembering it was time for her pious devotions.

It was a little game that Emily became good at.

1 Kings 8:22–23, 27–30
Psalm 84
Mark 7:1–13

Wednesday

FEBRUARY 11

• OUR LADY OF LOURDES •

"The report I heard in my country about your deeds and your wisdom is true," she told the king. "Though I did not believe the report until I came and saw with my own eyes, I have discovered that they were not telling me the half. Your wisdom and prosperity surpass the report I heard."

—1 KINGS 10:6–7

The queen of Sheba was acclaimed for her wealth and wisdom, but when she saw King Solomon's superior achievements, she gave him her ungrudging praise.

Do I acknowledge other people's gifts with the same freedom and generosity of spirit? Or do I sometimes feel so threatened that I withhold applause?

1 Kings 10:1–10
Psalm 37
Mark 7:14–23

Thursday

FEBRUARY 12

• LINCOLN'S BIRTHDAY •

The woman ... begged him to drive the demon out of her daughter. He said to her, "Let the children be fed first."

—MARK 7:26–27

It wasn't the first time that Jesus had rebuffed an importunate request. "Woman, . . . [m]y hour has not yet come," he had told his own mother (John 2:4).

Now, another woman wanted to fast-forward Jesus' timetable. She couldn't afford to wait for the day when the gospel would be announced to non-Jews. Her suffering daughter needed a crumb *now,* not a feast later!

Did Jesus think of his mother as he gave the Syrophoenician woman the reward of her faith?

1 Kings 11:4–13
Psalm 106
Mark 7:24–30

Friday

FEBRUARY 13

But my people did not listen to my words;
Israel did not obey me.
So I gave them over to hardness of heart;
they followed their own designs.
—PSALM 81:12–13

When you stop your ears to the still, small voice of conscience, you put yourself at the mercy of your own shortsighted counsel.

1 Kings 11:29–32; 12:19
Psalm 81
Mark 7:31–37

Saturday

FEBRUARY 14

• SAINT CYRIL, MONK • SAINT METHODIUS, BISHOP • VALENTINE'S DAY •

At Horeb they fashioned a calf,
worshiped a metal statue.
They exchanged their glorious God
for the image of a grass-eating bull.
—PSALM 106:19–20

Rick and Janet left the church because they found it "too much of a stretch" to believe in things like miracles and the real presence of Jesus in the Eucharist. They have no problem putting their faith in the power of crystals and healing energy circles, however.

1 Kings 12:26–32; 13:33–34
Psalm 106
Mark 8:1–10

Sunday

FEBRUARY 15

Rejoice and leap for joy on that day!

—LUKE 6:23

Joanna thought there'd be a team of four to clean up after the parish potluck dinner, but she discovered that she and Michael were the only ones who had volunteered. Sister Rose got the copy for the parish bulletin so late that she had to stay up till midnight to get it done on time. Ninety-nine percent of the parents were delighted with the first-communion program, but 99 percent of the feedback to its director came from the disgruntled 1 percent.

Even in small inconveniences and frustrations, there are hidden invitations to "rejoice and leap for joy!" Do we look for them?

Jeremiah 17:5–8
Psalm 1
1 Corinthians 15:12, 16–20
Luke 6:17, 20–26

Monday

FEBRUARY 16

• PRESIDENTS' DAY •

For the sun comes up with its scorching heat and dries up the grass, its flower droops, and the beauty of its appearance vanishes. So will the rich person fade away in the midst of his pursuits.

—JAMES 1:11

Plans and activities can give the illusion of lively growth and progress, but they can't substitute for the real thing. Eighty-year-old Mr. Flint, sitting in his wheelchair in the nursing-home dining room, may be far more alive than the influential, globetrotting diplomat. It all depends on what life sources they're tapping into.

James 1:1–11
Psalm 119
Mark 8:11–13

Tuesday

FEBRUARY 17

• THE SEVEN FOUNDERS OF THE ORDER OF SERVITES, RELIGIOUS •

When I say, "My foot is slipping,"
your love, LORD, holds me up.
—PSALM 94:18

You're the steel-belted radials for the icy stretches of my life, the sturdy hiking boots on the rough trails, the precision skis that grip the difficult slopes. Held firmly in your love, I can hold firmly to the course that lies ahead.

James 1:12–18
Psalm 94
Mark 8:14–21

Wednesday

FEBRUARY 18

[Jesus] took the blind man by the hand and led him outside the village. . . . Then he laid hands on his eyes a second time and he saw clearly; his sight was restored and he could see everything distinctly. Then he sent him home and said, "Do not even go into the village."

—MARK 8:23, 25–26

Julie finally realized that her social environment was fostering her negative, self-centered outlook on life and was affecting her values. The realization was the easy part. Then came the challenge of making hard decisions about whom she should be spending her time with now.

James 1:19–27
Psalm 15
Mark 8:22–26

Thursday

FEBRUARY 19

My brothers, show no partiality as you adhere to the faith in our glorious Lord Jesus Christ. . . . [I]f you fulfill the royal law according to the scripture, "You shall love your neighbor as yourself," you are doing well. But if you show partiality, you commit sin, and are convicted by the law as transgressors.

—JAMES 2:1, 8–9

Love means . . . never listening more carefully to a celebrity than to a "nobody" . . . never treating those who didn't give a dime to the capital campaign with less respect than the big donors get . . . never estimating the executives in the office building to be of greater worth than the people who vacuum the hallways at night.

Anything else is self-interest, not love.

James 2:1–9
Psalm 34
Mark 8:27–33

Friday

FEBRUARY 20

Do you want proof, you ignoramus, that faith without works is useless?

—JAMES 2:20

No member of an environmentalist society would betray his or her founder's principles by advocating the destruction of the rain forest. No disciple of Martin Luther King Jr. would use terrorist tactics to advance a just cause.

So how can we say we have faith in—and therefore have a close relationship with—a God who loves poor people, while neglecting to show that love in action? If faith has made you a follower of Jesus, you demonstrate it by your works of mercy. To claim that action is optional, says James, is nothing short of stupid.

James 2:14–24, 26
Psalm 112
Mark 8:34–9:1

Saturday

FEBRUARY 21

• SAINT PETER DAMIAN, BISHOP AND DOCTOR OF THE CHURCH •

[W]e all fall short in many respects. If anyone does not fall short in speech, he is a perfect man, able to bridle his whole body also.

—JAMES 3:2

Anna and Virginia's plaintive appeal wafted downstairs to where the rest of us were finishing dinner. "Don't anyone laugh or say anything mean." Then they slunk into the dining room, modeling the shiny polyester skirts and vests they would have to wear at their new high school. Our promise was immediately put to the test: the uniforms were truly unflattering.

"Don't anyone laugh or say anything mean" has become a family slogan—and one I often invoke in my own personal battle to tame my tongue.

James 3:1–10
Psalm 12
Mark 9:2–13

Sunday

FEBRUARY 22

• WASHINGTON'S BIRTHDAY •

Give and gifts will be given to you; a good measure, packed together, shaken down, and overflowing, will be poured into your lap. For the measure with which you measure will in return be measured out to you.

—LUKE 6:38

If we want to drink from the river of God's love, we have to help others drink from it too.

Unless we step into the flow of divine generosity and channel it to others, we'll always be dry and thirsty.

1 Samuel 26:2, 7–9, 12–13, 22–23
Psalm 103
1 Corinthians 15:45–49
Luke 6:27–38

Monday

FEBRUARY 23

• SAINT POLYCARP, BISHOP AND MARTYR •

When he entered the house, his disciples asked him in private, "Why could we not drive it out?" He said to them, "This kind can only come out through prayer."

—MARK 9:28–29

The volunteer counselors at the crisis pregnancy center were knowledgeable, well-trained, and committed. Even more important, they thought, was that they had behind-the-scenes support from a group of prayer partners, whose regular intercession they relied on. As they all knew, staying connected to Jesus is the only way to receive power and help for serving others in his name.

James 3:13–18
Psalm 19
Mark 9:14–29

Tuesday

FEBRUARY 24

Resist the devil, and he will flee from you.

—JAMES 4:7

When you're facing temptation, St. Ignatius Loyola advises in his *Spiritual Exercises,* "do not yield an inch. The enemy is weak when faced by firmness but strong in the face of acquiescence."

Any lion tamer would understand the logic of this approach.

James 4:1–10
Psalm 55
Mark 9:30–37

Wednesday

FEBRUARY 25

• ASH WEDNESDAY •

Yet even now, says the LORD,
return to me with your whole heart,
with fasting, and weeping, and mourning.
—JOEL 2:12

This is all wrong, Lord. It's disturbing. If there's any pleading to be done, I'm the one who should do it. After all, I'm the one who jeopardized our relationship, not you. Besides, don't you care about your dignity and position? You're the ruler of heaven and earth . . . Who am I?

Why do you bother? Why do you pursue me? I'm almost beginning to believe that there's something serious at stake.

Joel 2:12–18
Psalm 51
2 Corinthians 5:20–6:2
Matthew 6:1–6, 16–18

Thursday

FEBRUARY 26

Then he said to all, "If anyone wishes to come after me, he must deny himself and take up his cross daily and follow me."

—LUKE 9:23

Taking up your cross is like buying a one-way ticket to your dream destination without knowing the itinerary. Will your journey lead over land or under water, into stagnant swamps or pleasant pastures, through rainy climates or desert ones? You just don't know. You will have a guide, though, someone who's been there before. That makes all the difference.

Deuteronomy 30:15–20
Psalm 1
Luke 9:22–25

Friday

FEBRUARY 27

Do you call this a fast,
a day acceptable to the LORD?
This, rather, is the fasting that I wish:
releasing those bound unjustly,
untying the thongs of the yoke;
Setting free the oppressed,
breaking every yoke;
Sharing your bread with the hungry,
sheltering the oppressed and the homeless;
Clothing the naked when you see them.

—ISAIAH 58:5–7

Whether it's on the public or the private scale, there's no worship without justice.

Isaiah 58:1–9
Psalm 51
Matthew 9:14–15

Saturday

FEBRUARY 28

The Pharisees and their scribes complained to his disciples, saying, "Why do you eat and drink with tax collectors and sinners?"

—LUKE 5:30

Once you start screening the guest list to filter out all the unworthies, you're not even going to be able to fill a table for two, let alone a banquet hall.

Isaiah 58:9–14
Psalm 86
Luke 5:27–32

Sunday

FEBRUARY 29

Then he led him to Jerusalem, made him stand on the parapet of the temple, and said to him, "If you are the Son of God, throw yourself down from here. . . ." Jesus said to him in reply, "It also says, 'You shall not put the Lord, your God, to the test.'"

—LUKE 4:9, 12

How offensive you must find it, Lord, my God, when I try to manipulate you into doing things my way, supporting my agenda, and just generally being at my beck and call. Forgive me for all the times I've treated you like a pack of super-power batteries I could just recharge to get me off and running in my own direction again.

Deuteronomy 26:4–10
Psalm 91
Romans 10:8–13
Luke 4:1–13

Monday

MARCH 1

I was . . . a stranger and you welcomed me.

—MATTHEW 25:35

I was traveling solo around France and missed the last train back to my hotel. As I stood on the darkening platform watching commuters rush away, I worried about what to do. Help came in the person of an Algerian immigrant, who arranged for my safe return and refused any compensation for his trouble. "Just remember this next time you hear someone speaking badly about Algerians," he said. I have remembered. Personally, I still have a lot to learn about his kind of hospitality.

Leviticus 19:1–2, 11–18
Psalm 19
Matthew 25:31–46

Tuesday

MARCH 2

This is how you are to pray:
Our Father in heaven . . .
—MATTHEW 6:9

The very first word of the most basic prayer in my repertoire reminds me that I come to God as a member of an incredibly large family. God is both *my* Father, who listens to me in a very intimate way, and *our* Father, who can give the same personal attention to six billion other children.

Isaiah 55:10–11
Psalm 34
Matthew 6:7–15

Wednesday MARCH 3

• SAINT KATHARINE DREXEL, VIRGIN •

Jonah began his journey through the city, and had gone but a single day's walk announcing, "Forty days more and Nineveh shall be destroyed," when the people of Nineveh believed God; they proclaimed a fast and all of them, great and small, put on sackcloth.

—JONAH 3:4–5

The Ninevites knew how to connect the dots. When confronted with the threat of imminent destruction, they were quick to figure out why they deserved it and how they needed to change in order to avoid it. Do we connect whatever dots we are given with anywhere near the same alacrity?

Jonah 3:1–10
Psalm 51
Luke 11:29–32

Thursday MARCH 4

• SAINT CASIMIR •

Do to others whatever you would have them do to you. This is the law and the prophets.

—MATTHEW 7:12

The transformation in Liz began when she changed the topic of the list she always carried around in her head. Instead of remembering the occasions when she was hurt or slighted, she decided to take note of the times when people went out of their way to show her kindness and generosity. Before long, Liz was looking for everyday opportunities to be that loving, generous kind of person herself.

Esther C:12, 14–16, 23–25
Psalm 138
Matthew 7:7–12

Friday

MARCH 5

Do I indeed derive any pleasure from the death of the wicked? says the Lord GOD. *Do I not rather rejoice when he turns from his evil way that he may live?*

—EZEKIEL 18:23

If I want to enter into the inconceivably glorious experience of God's joy in the future, I will give God occasion for joy in the present.

Ezekiel 18:21–28
Psalm 130
Matthew 5:20–26

Saturday

MARCH 6

Today you are making this agreement with the LORD: he is to be your God and you are to walk in his ways and observe his statutes, commandments and decrees, and to hearken to his voice.

—DEUTERONOMY 26:17

Yes, Father, you are my God, and I gratefully renew my agreement with you today!

I will follow your Son as he teaches me to walk in your ways and observe your commands.

I will listen attentively for your Holy Spirit, who counsels and strengthens me.

Help me to live this day in a way that will make others want to become your children too.

Deuteronomy 26:16–19
Psalm 119
Matthew 5:43–48

Sunday

MARCH 7

Join with others in being imitators of me, brothers, and observe those who thus conduct themselves according to the model you have in us.

—PHILIPPIANS 3:17

The only people who can safely say, "Be like me" are those who can also say, "I live, no longer I, but Christ lives in me" (Galatians 2:20).

Genesis 15:5–12, 17–18
Psalm 27
Philippians 3:17–4:1 or 3:20–4:1
Luke 9:28–36

Monday

MARCH 8

• SAINT JOHN OF GOD, RELIGIOUS •

Justice, O Lord, is on your side; we are shamefaced even to this day. . . . O LORD, we are shamefaced, like our kings, our princes, and our fathers, for having sinned against you. . . . [W]e rebelled against you and paid no heed to your command, O LORD, our God, to live by the law you gave us through your servants the prophets.

—DANIEL 9:7–10

You could have protested your innocence, Daniel. You could have played the "me versus them" blame game. After all, *you* weren't the one who had offended God; it was the "kings, princes, and fathers"! So why did you pray so repentantly, as if you stood in solidarity with these sinners? Surely your sins were nothing like theirs! Why didn't you dissociate yourself from these people?

And why does your prayer bother me so much?

Daniel 9:4–10
Psalm 79
Luke 6:36–38

Tuesday MARCH 9

• SAINT FRANCES OF ROME, RELIGIOUS •

[C]ease doing evil; learn to do good.
Make justice your aim: redress the wronged,
hear the orphan's plea, defend the widow.
—ISAIAH 1:16–17

Many people live in desperate need of the justice that Christ will bring when he comes again in glory. Do I know any of them? Do I know *of* any of them? Is there something I can do—in my family, parish, neighborhood, school, workplace, or beyond—to help someone get the just treatment they deserve?

Isaiah 1:10, 16–20
Psalm 50
Matthew 23:1–12

Wednesday

MARCH 10

Then the mother of the sons of Zebedee approached him with her sons and did him homage, wishing to ask him for something. . . . "Command that these two sons of mine sit, one at your right and the other at your left, in your kingdom."

—MATTHEW 20:20–21

After three years of intensive discipleship training, James and John hadn't grasped the essentials of Jesus' teaching about the kingdom and how to enter it. They did seem to have noticed, though, that their master usually said yes to requests for help from middle-aged women. "Go ahead, Mom, you ask him. He'll listen to you."

Ignorance, manipulation, and the pursuit of self-centered ambitions—doesn't Jesus have to deal with these in his present-day followers too?

Jeremiah 18:18–20
Psalm 31
Matthew 20:17–28

Thursday

MARCH 11

Happy those who do not follow
the counsel of the wicked,
Nor go the way of sinners,
nor sit in company with scoffers.

—PSALM 1:1

Happy those who take their advice
from counselors wise in the Spirit,
who move along the narrow road
in the company of Christ's followers,
who spend their time with people
who pursue "whatever is true" and honorable
(Philippians 4:8).

Happy those who find friends
to point them to the law and love of the Lord.

Jeremiah 17:5–10
Psalm 1
Luke 16:19–31

Friday

MARCH 12

When [Joseph's] brothers saw that their father loved him best of all his sons, they hated him so much that they would not even greet him.

—GENESIS 37:4

The church fathers viewed envy as *the* diabolical sin. St. John Vianney offered one reason why: "In the same way that the devil after his fall felt, and still feels, extreme anger at seeing us the heirs of the glory of the good God, so the envious person feels sadness at seeing the spiritual and temporal prosperity of their neighbor." When we give in to envy, we walk "in the footsteps of the devil."

Genesis 37:3–4, 12–13, 17–28
Psalm 105
Matthew 21:33–43, 45–46

Saturday

MARCH 13

Bless the LORD, my soul;
all my being, bless his holy name!
Bless the LORD, my soul;
do not forget all the gifts of God.
—PSALM 103:1–2

When it comes to cultivating a spirit of gratitude, half the battle is remembering what we're grateful for.

Micah 7:14–15, 18–20
Psalm 103
Luke 15:1–3, 11–32

Sunday
MARCH 14

God called out to him from the bush, "Moses! Moses! . . . Come no nearer! Remove the sandals from your feet, for the place where you stand is holy ground. I am the God of your father, . . . the God of Abraham, the God of Isaac, the God of Jacob."

—EXODUS 3:4–6

As I walked home from work mulling over how to ward off a friend's demands on my time, God broke into my thoughts. It was an invitation to repent of some recent selfish behavior, but it was issued so mercifully that I was overwhelmed. To me, the stretch of sidewalk where that revelation took place is holy ground—and, quite literally, a concrete reminder of God's forgiving love.

Exodus 3:1–8, 13–15
Psalm 103
1 Corinthians 10:1–6, 10–12
Luke 13:1–9

Monday

MARCH 15

But Naaman went away angry, saying, "I thought that [Elisha] would surely come out and stand there to invoke the LORD his God, and would move his hand over the spot, and thus cure the leprosy." . . . But his servants came up and reasoned with him. "My father," they said, "if the prophet had told you to do something extraordinary, would you not have done it? All the more now, since he said to you, 'Wash and be clean,' should you do as he said."

—2 KINGS 5:11, 13

Naaman was undoubtedly better educated and more worldly-wise than his servants, but they were the ones with the common sense. Wisdom often speaks through seemingly unlikely instruments.

2 Kings 5:1–15
Psalm 42
Luke 4:24–30

Tuesday

MARCH 16

Then Peter approaching asked him, "Lord, if my brother sins against me, how often must I forgive him? As many as seven times?" Jesus answered, "I say to you, not seven times but seventy-seven times."

—MATTHEW 18:21–22

The only way to stop your vengefulness from escalating is to escalate the rate of your forgiveness—to infinity.

Daniel 3:25, 34–43
Psalm 25
Matthew 18:21–35

Wednesday MARCH 17

• ST. PATRICK'S DAY •

[W]hat great nation has statutes and decrees that are as just as this whole law which I am setting before you today? However, take care and be earnestly on your guard not to forget the things which your own eyes have seen, nor let them slip from your memory as long as you live, but teach them to your children and to your children's children.

—DEUTERONOMY 4:8–9

I will open my heart to your commands, Lord, for you speak words of life. I will spend more time sitting at your feet and absorbing your teachings. Give me wisdom and understanding as I pledge myself to following your ways and teaching them to others.

And now, what practical steps will I take to remember these good resolutions?

Deuteronomy 4:1, 5–9
Psalm 147
Matthew 5:17–19

Thursday

MARCH 18

• SAINT CYRIL OF JERUSALEM, BISHOP AND DOCTOR OF THE CHURCH •

Whoever is not with me is against me, and whoever does not gather with me scatters.

—LUKE 11:23

Scott prided himself on being an impartial seeker of truth. He gave an attentive hearing to both sides of an argument. He withheld judgment on issues and events, pending further information. In the end, though, Scott never did move from observing to participating in the business of life. He was too comfortable searching to take on the risk of committing to whatever truth he found.

Jeremiah 7:23–28
Psalm 95
Luke 11:14–23

Friday MARCH 19

• SAINT JOSEPH, HUSBAND OF THE BLESSED VIRGIN MARY •

When Joseph awoke, he did as the angel of the Lord had commanded him and took his wife into his home.

—MATTHEW 1:24

Joseph didn't say yes to God in so many words. He didn't have to. His actions—like those of the wise carpenter who built his house on rock—said it all.

2 Samuel 7:4–5, 12–14, 16
Psalm 89
Romans 4:13, 16–18, 22
Matthew 1:16, 18–21, 24 or Luke 2:41–51

Saturday

MARCH 20

He then addressed this parable to those who were convinced of their own righteousness and despised everyone else. "Two people went up to the temple area to pray; one was a Pharisee and the other was a tax collector . . ."

—LUKE 18:9–10

If I'm quick to deplore other people's pride and to promote myself into the ranks of the humble, perhaps I should examine whether I'm really just a Pharisee dressed in tax collectors' clothing.

Hosea 6:1–6
Psalm 51
Luke 18:9–14

Sunday

MARCH 21

His son said to him, "Father, I have sinned against heaven and against you; I no longer deserve to be called your son." But his father ordered his servants, "Quickly bring the finest robe and put it on him. . . . Then let us celebrate with a feast."

—LUKE 15:21–23

I go to you with a repentant heart, though knowing full well that my motives are mixed and that my prayer of contrition cannot cancel out my offense.

But always, Father, your love undoes me. You cut short my little speech. You hurry to welcome me with the white robe of salvation, with loving signs of acceptance.

In your house, repentance always leads to celebration.

Joshua 5:9–12
Psalm 34
2 Corinthians 5:17–21
Luke 15:1–3, 11–32

Monday

MARCH 22

You changed my mourning into dancing. . . .
O LORD, my God,
forever will I give you thanks.
—PSALM 30:12–13

Thinking she was only six weeks pregnant and having a miscarriage, a woman I know wept all the way to the hospital . . . where she discovered that she had wildly miscalculated. She wasn't miscarrying at all: her pregnancy had come to term and she was in labor. She didn't fully believe it, though, until eight-pound Naomi was put into her arms. Then the dancing began.

Isaiah 65:17–21
Psalm 30
John 4:43–54

Tuesday MARCH 23

• SAINT TURIBIUS DE MOGROVEJO, BISHOP •

When Jesus saw him lying there and knew that he had been ill for a long time, he said to him, "Do you want to be well?" The sick man answered him, "Sir, I have no one to put me into the pool when the water is stirred up; while I am on my way, someone else gets down there before me."

—JOHN 5:6–7

Why didn't the paralyzed man give Jesus a straight answer? Didn't he want to be healed? After thirty-eight years of being an invalid, did he prefer a familiar illness to the responsibilities that come with wellness?

I can see myself in this self-pitying invalid. Jesus, help me to accept the total health package you offer me—even when I feel intimidated by the accompanying responsibilities. Yes, Jesus, I *do* want to be well, body and soul!

Ezekiel 47:1–9, 12
Psalm 46
John 5:1–16

Wednesday

MARCH 24

Do not be amazed at this, because the hour is coming in which all who are in the tombs will hear his voice and will come out, those who have done good deeds to the resurrection of life, but those who have done wicked deeds to the resurrection of condemnation.

—JOHN 5:28–29

"He looks good," we say. "So peaceful, like he's about to wake up." Or, when the mortician has been more challenged, "She doesn't look like herself." Either way, as we know only too well, the body in the casket is utterly without life.

And yet these lifeless bodies will one day hear and respond to their Redeemer's voice. We must believe this. Because "if for this life only we have hoped in Christ, we are the most pitiable people of all" (1 Corinthians 15:19).

Isaiah 49:8–15
Psalm 145
John 5:17–30

Thursday MARCH 25

• THE ANNUNCIATION OF THE LORD •

I said, "Here I am. . . .
To do your will is my delight." . . .
Your deed I did not hide within my heart;
your loyal deliverance I have proclaimed.
I made no secret of your enduring kindness
to a great assembly.

—PSALM 40:8–9, 11

She gave her humble yes in a moment of personal prayer and spoke her magnificent praise of God in a conversation with a relative. How could Mary have guessed that both declarations would resound eternally to God's glory in the vast assembly of the church?

Isaiah 7:10–14; 8:10
Psalm 40
Hebrews 10:4–10
Luke 1:26–38

Friday

MARCH 26

[The wicked] said among themselves, thinking not aright: . . .
"Let us beset the just one, because he is obnoxious to us. . . .
To us he is the censure of our thoughts."

—WISDOM 2:1, 12, 14

It's not always a conscious decision. And it's hardly ever labeled "wicked." In fact, the worst persecutors of holy people like Bernadette, Padre Pio, and Mary MacKillop were religious superiors who persuaded themselves that they were doing good.

Lord, you who know my mind and heart, expose my hidden motivations and make me docile to the prophets you send. When I'm persecuting you in my thoughts and in my words, let me know it—and don't let me get away with murder.

Wisdom 2:1, 12–22
Psalm 34
John 7:1–2, 10, 25–30

Saturday

MARCH 27

So the guards went to the chief priests and Pharisees, who asked them, "Why did you not bring him?" The guards answered, "Never before has anyone spoken like this one."

—JOHN 7:45–46

The temple guards didn't normally go around disobeying orders. But unlike the priests and Pharisees, they found it impossible to carry on with business as usual when they came face to face with Jesus.

Every day, in every part of the world, Jesus still evokes astonishment and wonder. If our experience of him has become routine, it's time to pray for the grace to be amazed.

Jeremiah 11:18–20
Psalm 7
John 7:40–53

Sunday

MARCH 28

See, I am doing something new!
Now it springs forth, do you not perceive it?
In the desert I make a way,
in the wasteland, rivers.

—ISAIAH 43:19

You drew beauty and order out of chaos at the dawn of time. You renew creation and rescue it from chaos at the dawn of the third millennium.

God of hope, renew us as we strain to perceive the signs of your now-and-coming kingdom.

Make your new ways and rivers known to us so that we may travel them with you!

Isaiah 43:16–21
Psalm 126
Philippians 3:8–14
John 8:1–11

Monday

MARCH 29

You guide me along the right path
for the sake of your name.
Even when I walk through a dark valley,
I fear no harm for you are at my side.

—PSALM 23:3–4

The fact that bad things happen to good people may shake our faith in God, but it never shook the psalmist's. He knew that a path can be "right" even when it leads through a "dark valley."

Daniel 13:1–9, 15–17, 19–30, 33–62 or 13:41–62
Psalm 23
John 8:12–20

Tuesday

MARCH 30

[T]he people complained against God and Moses, "Why have you brought us up from Egypt to die in this desert, where there is no food or water? We are disgusted with this wretched food!"

—NUMBERS 21:5

In the family room, the children were telling silly jokes and recording them on a beat-up tape recorder. Nearby in the kitchen, Ann Marie was telling a friend about her latest problems with her new house and her in-laws.

Later, listening to the children's tape and hearing her own voice in the background, she was startled. Did she really sound so peevish? Did her tone match her troubles—which were minor, really? Did her gripes even make sense?

Numbers 21:4–9
Psalm 102
John 8:21–30

Wednesday MARCH 31

[Y]ou will know the truth, and the truth will set you free.

—JOHN 8:32

It lasted about four minutes, but to my sixth-grade self, that public piano recital felt like a forty-year agony. There I was, onstage, stuck on a movement of Beethoven's "Für Elise," playing it over and over again because I couldn't remember how to move on. My inattention to practice and memorization had caught up with me.

Lord, don't let me remain as stuck in my sins as I was in that piano piece. Your truth has given me a way out. Help me to take it!

Daniel 3:14–20, 91–92, 95
Daniel 3:52–56
John 8:31–42

Thursday

APRIL 1

No longer shall you be called Abram; your name shall be Abraham, for I am making you the father of a host of nations. I will render you exceedingly fertile; I will make nations of you; kings shall stem from you.

—GENESIS 17:5–6

When Christ's promised peace seems elusive,
when his kingdom seems threatened and his coming delayed,
when death and darkness seem to have won,
then I will think of you, Father Abraham,
who, without ever seeing God's promises to you realized in full,
believed to the end
and received the reward of your faith.

Genesis 17:3–9
Psalm 105
John 8:51–59

Friday APRIL 2

• SAINT FRANCIS OF PAOLA, HERMIT •

He said:
I love you, LORD, *my strength,*
LORD, *my rock, my fortress, my deliverer,*
My God, my rock of refuge,
my shield, my saving horn, my stronghold!
—PSALM 18:2–3

Love sparks the imagination and inspires a multitude of creative descriptions of the beloved.

Today, try turning your imagination loose as you think about the Lord. What concrete images would you choose to describe how you experience his help and presence in your life?

Jeremiah 20:10–13
Psalm 18
John 10:31–42

Saturday

APRIL 3

My dwelling shall be with them; I will be their God, and they shall be my people.

—EZEKIEL 37:27

After receiving communion, one devout response is to kneel down and close your eyes. Another one is to look around and give praise that Ezekiel's prophecy has been fulfilled: truly, God is dwelling with his people!

Ezekiel 37:21–28
Jeremiah 31:10–13
John 11:45–56

Sunday

APRIL 4

• PALM SUNDAY OF THE LORD'S PASSION • DAYLIGHT SAVING TIME BEGINS •

[Christ Jesus], though he was in the form of God,
did not regard equality with God something to be grasped.
Rather, he emptied himself,
taking the form of a slave.
—PHILIPPIANS 2:6–7

On the night of Palm Sunday, 1212, eighteen-year-old Clare of Assisi slipped out of the family castle to meet St. Francis and the brothers, who received her into consecrated religious life. Clare's first biographer said she "gave the world a bill of divorce" because she wished to imitate Christ in his poverty and self-emptying.

Given my circumstances, what must I leave behind to empty myself?

Luke 19:28–40
Isaiah 50:4–7
Psalm 22
Philippians 2:6–11
Luke 22:14–23:56 or 23:1–49

Monday

APRIL 5

Six days before Passover Jesus came to Bethany, where Lazarus was, whom Jesus had raised from the dead. They gave a dinner for him there, and Martha served, while Lazarus was one of those reclining at table with him.

—JOHN 12:1–2

By all rights, Lazarus should have been reclining in the tomb. Instead, he reclined side by side with the Lord of life, whom the tomb cannot contain. And to think that this is our destiny too!

Isaiah 42:1–7
Psalm 27
John 12:1–11

Tuesday

APRIL 6

Though I thought I had toiled in vain,
and for nothing, uselessly, spent my strength,
Yet my reward is with the LORD,
my recompense is with my God.
—ISAIAH 49:4

After an air raid on Stuttgart during World War II, Pastor Helmut Thielicke walked around his neighborhood in utter gloom. His church was rubble, his congregation scattered. As he stood looking into a bombed-out cellar, a woman came up. "My husband died in there," she said. And then: "He and I were in the cathedral church the last time you preached. And here before this pit I want to thank you for preparing him for eternity." It was a sudden glimpse into God's hidden kingdom.

Isaiah 49:1–6
Psalm 71
John 13:21–33, 36–38

Wednesday

APRIL 7

The Son of Man indeed goes, as it is written of him, but woe to that man by whom the Son of Man is betrayed. It would be better for that man if he had never been born.

—MATTHEW 26:24

At every eucharistic liturgy, Byzantine Rite Catholics recite a prayer that includes the line "I will not betray you with a kiss, as did Judas."

I always couple that bold promise with a private appeal for God's mercy: "Help me, my Savior, for you know that without your help I will *certainly* 'betray you with a kiss, as did Judas.'"

Isaiah 50:4–9
Psalm 69
Matthew 26:14–25

Thursday APRIL 8

• HOLY THURSDAY •

[D]uring supper, fully aware that the Father had put everything into his power and that he had come from God and was returning to God, he rose from supper and took off his outer garments. He took a towel and tied it around his waist. Then he poured water into a basin and began to wash the disciples' feet and dry them with the towel around his waist.

—JOHN 13:2–5

When we see Jesus washing the disciples' feet, we understand the spirit in which he accepted death on the cross: both are acts of service, expressions of loving, personal care. When we put the image of the foot washing side by side with the crucifix, the one sheds light on the other.

Chrism Mass:
Isaiah 61:1–3, 6, 8–9
Psalm 89
Revelation 1:5–8
Luke 4:16–21

Lord's Supper:
Exodus 12:1–8, 11–14
Psalm 116
1 Corinthians 11:23–26
John 13:1–15

Friday
APRIL 9

• GOOD FRIDAY OF THE LORD'S PASSION •

After this, Joseph of Arimathea, secretly a disciple of Jesus for fear of the Jews, asked Pilate if he could remove the body of Jesus. And Pilate permitted it. So he came and took his body. Nicodemus, the one who had first come to him at night, also came bringing a mixture of myrrh and aloes weighing about one hundred pounds. They took the body of Jesus and bound it with burial cloths along with the spices, according to the Jewish burial custom.

—JOHN 19:38–40

When confronted with the cross, most people turn away. But always there are some who stand before Jesus crucified and discover courage they didn't know they had to declare themselves disciples.

Where in my life do I most need that courage now?

Isaiah 52:13–53:12
Psalm 31
Hebrews 4:14–16; 5:7–9
John 18:1–19:42

Saturday APRIL 10

• HOLY SATURDAY •

[T]he Israelites marched into the midst of the sea on dry land, with the water like a wall to their right and to their left.

—EXODUS 14:22

This is the night when the hand that rolled back the waters will roll away the stone. O holy night! O holy Lord, whom the grave cannot contain!

Genesis 1:1–2:2 or 1:1, 26–31
Psalm 104 or Psalm 33
Genesis 22:1–18 or 22:1–2, 9–13, 15–18
Psalm 16
Exodus 14:15–15:1
Exodus 15:1–6, 17–18
Isaiah 54:5–14
Psalm 30
Isaiah 55:1–11
Baruch 3:9–15, 32–4:4
Psalm 19
Ezekiel 36:16–28
Psalms 42; 43 or Isaiah 12:2–6 or Psalm 51
Romans 6:3–11
Psalm 118
Luke 24:1–12

Sunday

APRIL 11

• EASTER SUNDAY • THE RESURRECTION OF THE LORD •

[B]ehold, two men in dazzling garments appeared to them. They were terrified and bowed their faces to the ground. They said to them, "Why do you seek the living one among the dead? He is not here, but he has been raised."

—LUKE 24:4–6

Kathy walked into the church, knelt down in the back pew, and looked around. Though she hadn't been to the shrine in ten years, every detail was etched in her mind—the play of light on the crucifix, the blues of Mary's stained-glass mantle, the mingled odors of incense and candle wax, the pilgrims streaming in and out. But most clearly of all, Kathy remembered how Jesus had unexpectedly broken into her life on that first visit. She had gone away transformed, filled with hope and burning love. Now she closed her eyes and waited for it to happen again. Nothing.

Later, Kathy got the message. She couldn't re-create her mountaintop experiences by revisiting the places where they had happened or by trying to recapture the thoughts and states of mind that had led up to them. They were gone. And since she had changed, what good would they have done? No, she had to let them go in trusting expectation of new meetings and mountaintops down the road. The other way was a dead end—Jesus doesn't live on memory lane.

Acts 10:34, 37–43
Psalm 118
Colossians 3:1–4 or 1 Corinthians 5:6–8
John 20:1–9 or Luke 24:1–12 or, at an afternoon or evening Mass, Luke 24:13–35

Monday APRIL 12

I keep the LORD always before me;
with the Lord at my right, I shall never be shaken.
Therefore my heart is glad, my soul rejoices;
my body also dwells secure,
For you will not abandon me to Sheol,
nor let your faithful servant see the pit.
—PSALM 16:8–10

In his Pentecost sermon, Peter recites these verses as if Jesus is praying them to the Father.

In our own prayer, we can recite them as if Jesus is praying them to the Father alongside us. We join our expression of faith to our Savior's, and his confidence reinforces our own.

Acts 2:14, 22–33
Psalm 16
Matthew 28:8–15

Tuesday

APRIL 13

"[G]o to my brothers and tell them, 'I am going to my Father and your Father, to my God and your God.'" Mary of Magdala went and announced to the disciples, "I have seen the Lord," and what he told her.

—JOHN 20:17–18

When the apostles preached Jesus risen from the dead, they knew from experience that it was a demanding message. To believe or not to believe? To take someone else's word or not? To reorient your life around an event that had been witnessed by many—but not by you?

The apostles' test of faith was brief. But thanks to that dark interval between hearing Mary's announcement and seeing Jesus alive, they are credible evangelists to those whose test of faith may last a lifetime.

Acts 2:36–41
Psalm 33
John 20:11–18

Wednesday

APRIL 14

[W]hile they were conversing and debating, Jesus himself drew near and walked with them, but their eyes were prevented from recognizing him.

—LUKE 24:15–16

There are people whose conversation refreshes, whose wisdom renews, whose insights shed light in unexpected ways. In their company, we sense the presence of an unseen party who sets hearts aflame.

Acts 3:1–10
Psalm 105
Luke 24:13–35

Thursday

APRIL 15

You denied the Holy and Righteous One and asked that a murderer be released to you.

—ACTS 3:14

If given a say about who should move into their apartment building, who in their right mind would choose Adolf Hitler over Mahatma Gandhi? Slobodan Milosević over Martin Luther King Jr.? Idi Amin over Mother Teresa?

It's no contest. So why do we keep the father of lies in the guest room when the Savior is waiting at the door?

Acts 3:11–26
Psalm 8
Luke 24:35–48

Friday

APRIL 16

So the disciple whom Jesus loved said to Peter, "It is the Lord."
—JOHN 21:7

Holy Spirit,
you who opened the eyes of the beloved disciple,
open my eyes as well.
Increase my love so that I will catch the signs
of my Lord's presence,
see him in all the ways he comes to me,
recognize his voice when he calls out,
and become so alert to his style and way of doing things
that I'll know when to alert others too.

Acts 4:1–12
Psalm 118
John 21:1–14

Saturday
APRIL 17

So they called them back and ordered them not to speak or teach at all in the name of Jesus. Peter and John, however, said to them in reply, "Whether it is right in the sight of God for us to obey you rather than God, you be the judges. It is impossible for us not to speak about what we have seen and heard."

—ACTS 4:18–20

When it comes to gossip and slander, "Let anything you hear die within you; / be assured it will not make you burst" (Sirach 19:9). But when the news has to do with your experience of God's saving deeds, better not keep it in!

Acts 4:13–21
Psalm 118
Mark 16:9–15

Sunday

APRIL 18

Then he said to Thomas, "Put your finger here and see my hands, and bring your hand and put it into my side, and do not be unbelieving, but believe." Thomas answered and said to him, "My Lord and my God!" Jesus said to him, "Have you come to believe because you have seen me? Blessed are those who have not seen and have believed."

—JOHN 20:27–29

Sometimes it's downright embarrassing to be given the signs you stubbornly demanded. Here's betting that Thomas went on to live the rest of his life determined to choose the higher way—believing without needing to see.

Acts 5:12–16
Psalm 118
Revelation 1:9–13, 17–19
John 20:19–31

Monday

APRIL 19

The wind blows where it wills, and you can hear the sound it makes, but you do not know where it comes from or where it goes; so it is with everyone who is born of the Spirit.

—JOHN 3:8

I know a young man who was abandoned by his father and left to the "care" of a mother who did drugs, brought a string of disreputable boyfriends into the house, and often kept her son waiting on the sidewalk as she disappeared into a bar. He grew up to become a strong Christian who kept in close contact with his mother and cared for her tenderly in her declining years.

O God of surprises, who can foretell or track your Spirit's comings and goings in a human life?

Acts 4:23–31
Psalm 2
John 3:1–8

Tuesday

APRIL 20

Jesus answered and said to [Nicodemus], "You are the teacher of Israel and you do not understand this? Amen, amen, I say to you, we speak of what we know and we testify to what we have seen, but you people do not accept our testimony. If I tell you about earthly things and you do not believe, how will you believe if I tell you about heavenly things?"

—JOHN 3:10–12

The best teachers are those who recognize their ignorance and who eagerly remain in Wisdom's classroom as lifelong learners.

Acts 4:32–37
Psalm 93
John 3:7–15

Wednesday

APRIL 21

• SAINT ANSELM, BISHOP AND DOCTOR OF THE CHURCH •

But during the night, the angel of the Lord opened the doors of the prison, led them out, and said, "Go and take your place in the temple area, and tell the people everything about this life."

—ACTS 5:19–20

When Christ broke the grip of sin and death, he smashed open the gates of a prison that's black beyond imagining. If we truly understood the freedom he offers, we'd be out there at our posts, eagerly devising ways to take our place in the new evangelization.

Acts 5:17–26
Psalm 34
John 3:16–21

Thursday APRIL 22

The LORD is close to the brokenhearted,
saves those whose spirit is crushed.
—PSALM 34:19

Obeying God does not guarantee that we'll never get our spirits crushed, but it does mean that the crushing will work to our greater advantage in the end.

Acts 5:27–33
Psalm 34
John 3:31–36

Friday

APRIL 23

• SAINT GEORGE, MARTYR • SAINT ADALBERT, BISHOP AND MARTYR •

Wait for the LORD, take courage;
be stouthearted, wait for the LORD!
—PSALM 27:14

Max and Tammy's twentysomething son was making a mess of his life again, but for once they weren't rushing in to cover for him. Though they felt grieved and helpless, they knew the time had come to stand back and simply pray for God to intervene.

Sometimes it's waiting—and not doing—that calls for courage.

Acts 5:34–42
Psalm 27
John 6:1–15

Saturday

APRIL 24

• SAINT FIDELIS OF SIGMARINGEN, PRIEST AND MARTYR •

At that time, as the number of disciples continued to grow, the Hellenists complained against the Hebrews because their widows were being neglected in the daily distribution. So the Twelve called together the community of the disciples.

—ACTS 6:1–2

When we can accept that even a church that was full of the Holy Spirit and led by saints could run into problems, then we can turn our attention from deploring our current church problems to finding effective processes for solving them.

Acts 6:1–7
Psalm 33
John 6:16–21

Sunday
APRIL 25

Then I heard every creature in heaven and on earth and under the earth
and in the sea, everything in the universe, cry out:
"To the one who sits on the throne and to the Lamb
be blessing and honor, glory and might,
forever and ever."
The four living creatures answered, "Amen," and the elders fell down
and worshiped.

—REVELATION 5:13–14

Every celebration of the Eucharist brings us into the never-ending liturgy of heaven. Caught up in the great hymn of the universe, we worship alongside saints and angels, unusual creatures and ordinary ones. And along with the twenty-four elders, we take off our crowns and bow in adoration before the enthroned Lamb of God.

Acts 5:27–32, 40–41
Psalm 30
Revelation 5:11–14
John 21:1–19 or 21:1–14

Monday

APRIL 26

Jesus answered them and said, "Amen, amen, I say to you, you are looking for me not because you saw signs but because you ate the loaves and were filled."

—JOHN 6:26

He'd had a rough life and no breaks. Often as he shuffled down the soup-kitchen line in the church basement, anger would get the best of him and he'd launch into bitter tirades. Then one day he caught a volunteer looking at him so compassionately that he stopped in midsentence. *Why does she come here and put up with me every week? What's in it for her?*

As he deciphered the signs, he was directed into a whole new way of living.

Acts 6:8–15
Psalm 119
John 6:22–29

Tuesday

APRIL 27

But they cried out in a loud voice, covered their ears, and rushed upon him together. They threw him out of the city, and began to stone him.

—ACTS 7:57–58

When Samantha was in high school, she hotly disputed her parents' "no boys in your bedroom" rule. It makes perfect sense to her now, though, as she raises her own teenage daughters—and counters their protests with patient explanations.

Acts 7:51–8:1
Psalm 31
John 6:30–35

Wednesday

APRIL 28

• SAINT PETER CHANEL, PRIEST AND MARTYR • SAINT LOUIS MARY DE MONTFORT, PRIEST •

Saul, meanwhile, was trying to destroy the church; entering house after house and dragging out men and women, he handed them over for imprisonment.

Now those who had been scattered went about preaching the word. Thus Philip went down to [the] city of Samaria and proclaimed the Messiah to them. With one accord, the crowds paid attention to what was said by Philip when they heard it and saw the signs he was doing. . . . There was great joy in that city.

—ACTS 8:3–6, 8

Even when it plays out during dark times, the Law of Unintended Consequences can result in some unexpectedly joyous developments. Just ask any World War II baby.

Acts 8:1–8
Psalm 66
John 6:35–40

Thursday

APRIL 29

• SAINT CATHERINE OF SIENA, VIRGIN AND DOCTOR OF THE CHURCH •

Then the angel of the Lord spoke to Philip, "Get up and head south on the road that goes down from Jerusalem to Gaza, the desert route." So he got up and set out. Now there was an Ethiopian eunuch, a court official of the Candace, that is, the queen of the Ethiopians, in charge of her entire treasury, who had come to Jerusalem to worship, and was returning home. Seated in his chariot, he was reading the prophet Isaiah.

—ACTS 8:26–28

Who ever would have thought that the rich guy in the fancy limo with the diplomatic plates would be interested in reading the Bible?

Acts 8:26–40
Psalm 66
John 6:44–51

Friday
APRIL 30

• SAINT PIUS V, POPE •

Jesus said to them, "Amen, amen, I say to you, unless you eat the flesh of the Son of Man and drink his blood, you do not have life within you. Whoever eats my flesh and drinks my blood has eternal life, and I will raise him on the last day."

—JOHN 6:53–54

Here is food that doesn't just sustain. It transforms those who partake of it and makes them into people who will never hunger or thirst again.

Jesus, bread of life, how wonderful you are!

Acts 9:1–20
Psalm 117
John 6:52–59

Saturday
MAY 1

• SAINT JOSEPH THE WORKER •

Peter sent them all out and knelt down and prayed. Then he turned to her body and said, "Tabitha, rise up." She opened her eyes, saw Peter, and sat up.

—ACTS 9:40

I once heard a story about a cancer patient whose doctor gave her six months to live. "Only God knows how much longer I have," she told the doctor. "Maybe he has more work for me to do." She went home to the care of a hospice nurse—and was so impressed by the woman that she went on to train as a hospice volunteer. As it turned out, she had seven more years of good works in her.

Acts 9:31–42
Psalm 116
John 6:60–69
or (for memorial):
Genesis 1:26–2:3 or Colossians 3:14–15, 17, 23–24
Psalm 90
Matthew 13:54–58

After this I had a vision of a great multitude, which no one could count, from every nation, race, people, and tongue. They stood before the throne and before the Lamb, wearing white robes and holding palm branches in their hands.

—REVELATION 7:9

The people who get to wave the palms in the heavenly courts are the ones who don't put them down when the joy of Palm Sunday gives way to the suffering of Good Friday. They are faithful witnesses, in good times and in bad.

Acts 13:14, 43–52
Psalm 100
Revelation 7:9, 14–17
John 10:27–30

Monday MAY 3

• SAINTS PHILIP AND JAMES, APOSTLES •

The heavens declare the glory of God.

—PSALM 19:2

I step out into an early summer twilight that twinkles with greenish flashes. On my right and on my left, fireflies hover and float up from the meadow to the treetops. The light display dazzles the mind as well as the eyes. Light-producing cells, nerve cells, nitric oxide, a mesh of oxygen-providing tubes—what complexity in these one-inch-long creatures!

The sun and moon declare God's glory, but even the smallest bodies in the heavens contribute praise in their own way.

1 Corinthians 15:1–8
Psalm 19
John 14:6–14

My sheep hear my voice; I know them, and they follow me.

—JOHN 10:27

"Hi, Dad."
"Hello, Meggie."
"This isn't Meggie."
"Oh. Hello, Maria."
"This isn't Maria."
"Anna? Virginia?"

When our daughters call and we confuse their voices, they give us a hard time about it. We're working on that—and working too on reducing the confusion we sometimes experience in calls from higher places.

Acts 11:19–26
Psalm 87
John 10:22–30

Wednesday MAY 5

While they were worshiping the Lord and fasting, the holy Spirit said, "Set apart for me Barnabas and Saul for the work to which I have called them."

—ACTS 13:2

The school year was beginning, so after Sunday Mass, Fr. Ed called the religious-education teachers to the front of the church for a special blessing.

It got Mike to wondering, as he sat there in his pew, about how he could contribute to the parish. Did God have anything special for him to do? Maybe he'd start praying to the Holy Spirit for direction and see if anything happened.

Acts 12:24–13:5
Psalm 67
John 12:44–50

The God of this people Israel chose our ancestors and exalted the people during their sojourn in the land of Egypt. With uplifted arms he led them out of it and for about forty years he put up with them in the desert.

—ACTS 13:17–18

He sure put up with a lot of complaints about the food. Even as they dined on miraculously supplied manna and quail, the people looked back to the leeks and onions and garlic they had enjoyed in Egypt. They'd been slaves there, mind you. But what's a life of hard labor compared to a familiar menu?

Am I like those picky eaters? Where is that complaining spirit alive in me? How do my gripes stack up against what God has done for me?

Acts 13:13–25
Psalm 89
John 13:16–20

Jesus said to him, "I am the way and the truth and the life."

—JOHN 14:6

Jesus didn't just set up the rescue ladder and walk away. He *is* the ladder, and he assists us to safety, rung by rung. What a relief for all of us who have a fear of heights!

Acts 13:26–33
Psalm 2
John 14:1–6

Sing a new song to the LORD.

—PSALM 98:1

Some days, I experience my prayer time the way the writer Flannery O'Connor said she experienced interviews: "I always feel like a dry cow being milked."

But there's this difference: just when I'm singing the same old tune, along comes the Holy Spirit to teach me something new.

Acts 13:44–52
Psalm 98
John 14:7–14

They strengthened the spirits of the disciples and exhorted them to persevere in the faith, saying, "It is necessary for us to undergo many hardships to enter the kingdom of God."

—ACTS 14:22

Why do hard truths come out sounding preachy and demoralizing when spoken by some people but life giving when spoken by others?

Acts 14:21–27
Psalm 145
Revelation 21:1–5
John 13:31–35

Monday
MAY 10

• BLESSED JOSEPH DE VEUSTER OF MOLOKAI (FATHER DAMIEN), PRIEST •

Not to us, LORD, not to us
but to your name give glory
because of your faithfulness and love.
—PSALM 115:1

Well, to tell you the truth, Lord, a teeny bit of glory would be nice. I think I could handle it. After all, don't I deserve *some* credit for my achievements? I've worked hard for you. I've been faithful. Why not do something to let other people know that you and I are close, that I'm a little bit—you know—holy? Of course, I'd give you all the credit. What about it, Lord?

Acts 14:5–18
Psalm 115
John 14:21–26

Peace I leave with you; my peace I give to you. Not as the world gives do I give it to you.

—JOHN 14:27

"You did the right thing," Claire's friends assured her. She had felt vaguely uncomfortable about how severely she had treated her new coworker, and her friends' encouragement eased her conscience and restored the luster to her self-image.

But it was a false peace. Claire's other coworkers, who knew the situation firsthand, would have rendered a different verdict.

Acts 14:19–28
Psalm 145
John 14:27–31

Wednesday MAY 12

• SAINTS NEREUS, ACHILLEUS, AND PANCRAS, MARTYRS •

Remain in me, as I remain in you.

—JOHN 15:4

Some of us seek high and low for you, as if we're on a scavenger hunt. Others, tipped off by that word *remain,* stay put and start digging. They've realized that you lie within, like buried treasure in a field.

Acts 15:1–6
Psalm 122
John 15:1–8

Thursday MAY 13

• OUR LADY OF FATIMA •

If you keep my commandments, you will remain in my love, just as I have kept my Father's commandments and remain in his love.

—JOHN 15:10

It's grace that admits us into God's house. But unless we learn the ways of obedience, we won't get to remain as permanent residents.

Acts 15:7–21
Psalm 96
John 15:9–11

Friday
MAY 14

• SAINT MATTHIAS, APOSTLE •

Then they prayed, "You, Lord, who know the hearts of all, show which one of these two you have chosen to take the place in this apostolic ministry from which Judas turned away to go to his own place." Then they gave lots to them, and the lot fell upon Matthias, and he was counted with the eleven apostles.

—ACTS 1:24–26

The Eleven were handpicked by Jesus, and Matthias was specially designated by the Holy Spirit. We may not always see it, but it works the same way with us. God is always the one who takes the initiative to call us home: "It was not you who chose me, but I who chose you" (John 15:16).

Acts 1:15–17, 20–26
Psalm 113
John 15:9–17

Saturday

MAY 15

• SAINT ISIDORE THE FARMER •

[W]orship the LORD with cries of gladness;
come before him with joyful song.
Know that the LORD is God,
our maker to whom we belong,
whose people we are.

—PSALM 100:2–3

God is like an expert craftsman whose fine workmanship comes with a guarantee to skillfully repair whatever the customer may break. Coming as we do from the hands of the Master Artisan, we can always find cause for joyful celebration—even on those cold gray mornings when we don't really feel like singing in the shower.

Acts 16:1–10
Psalm 100
John 15:18–21

Sunday
MAY 16

I saw no temple in the city, for its temple is the Lord God almighty and the Lamb. The city had no need of sun or moon to shine on it, for the glory of God gave it light, and its lamp was the Lamb.

—REVELATION 21:22–23

There were no churches, shrines, statues, icons, or stained-glass windows, no missalettes or prayer books. All that had passed away. God was immediately and totally present to each person, and there was no more need for mediation.

Acts 15:1–2, 22–29
Psalm 67
Revelation 21:10–14, 22–23
John 14:23–29

Monday
MAY 17

On the sabbath we went outside the city gate along the river where we thought there would be a place of prayer. We sat and spoke with the women who had gathered there. One of them, a woman named Lydia, a dealer in purple cloth, from the city of Thyatira, a worshiper of God, listened, and the Lord opened her heart to pay attention to what Paul was saying.

—ACTS 16:13–14

Lord, I know you've put some Lydias in my life. Help me to find them. Show me where to look and how to recognize these people whose hearts you have prepared. And when I sit down to talk with them, give me the words that will point them to you.

Acts 16:11–15
Psalm 149
John 15:26–16:4

Tuesday MAY 18

• SAINT JOHN I, POPE AND MARTYR •

About midnight, . . . Paul and Silas were praying and singing hymns to God as the prisoners listened.

—ACTS 16:25

They'd been roughed up by a mob and thrown into a maximum-security cell, where their feet were tied to a stake. It was probably discomfort that kept them awake late into the night, not a desire to keep vigil. They did have a choice, though, about how to spend the wakeful, uncomfortable hours.

Something to keep in mind the next time I'm on a long car trip or snowed in at the airport: praying and hymn singing are always options.

Acts 16:22–34
Psalm 138
John 16:5–11

Wednesday
MAY 19

I have much more to tell you, but you cannot bear it now. But when he comes, the Spirit of truth, he will guide you to all truth.

—JOHN 16:12–13

My husband and I are at the very beginning of learning Arabic. As I struggle to produce the unfamiliar sounds and script, I'm glad we have a wise, experienced tutor who knows just how much newness we neophytes can bear.

Holy Spirit, wisest of teachers, thank you for your patient, ongoing, one-step-at-a-time unfolding of God's revelation.

Acts 17:15, 22–18:1
Psalm 148
John 16:12–15

Thursday MAY 20

• THE ASCENSION OF THE LORD •

God mounts the throne amid shouts of joy;
the LORD, *amid trumpet blasts.*
Sing praise to God, sing praise;
sing praise to our king, sing praise.
—PSALM 47:6–7

If you've ever wondered what was happening on the other side of the cloud that took Jesus from the disciples' sight, this is it.

The Lamb is enthroned in the heavenly courts! The eternal banquet has begun, and one day we'll be sitting at that table too. Sing praise!

Acts 1:1–11
Psalm 47
Ephesians 1:17–23 or Hebrews 9:24–28; 10:19–23
Luke 24:46–53

Friday

MAY 21

• SAINT CHRISTOPHER MAGALLANES, PRIEST, AND HIS COMPANIONS, MARTYRS •

But I will see you again, and your hearts will rejoice, and no one will take your joy away from you. On that day you will not question me about anything.

—JOHN 16:22–23

The apostles must have been encouraged by the thought that they would see Jesus again one day. And perhaps Jesus was encouraged by the thought that he wouldn't have to deal with their questions for much longer.

As for our own obtuse questions—that's where the Holy Spirit comes in.

Acts 18:9–18
Psalm 47
John 16:20–23

Saturday

MAY 22

• SAINT RITA OF CASCIA, RELIGIOUS •

A Jew named Apollos, a native of Alexandria, an eloquent speaker, arrived in Ephesus. He was an authority on the scriptures. He had been instructed in the Way of the Lord and, with ardent spirit, spoke and taught accurately about Jesus, although he knew only the baptism of John. He began to speak boldly in the synagogue; but when Priscilla and Aquila heard him, they took him aside and explained to him the Way [of God] more accurately.

—ACTS 18:24–26

The husband-and-wife evangelization team could have felt threatened and intimidated by the convert with the attention-getting style. Instead, they took him under their wing and saw to it that his splendid gifts became even more effective.

Acts 18:23–28
Psalm 47
John 16:23–28

The Spirit and the bride say, "Come." Let the hearer say, "Come." Let the one who thirsts come forward, and the one who wants it receive the gift of life-giving water. . . .
The one who gives this testimony says, "Yes, I am coming soon." Amen! Come, Lord Jesus!

—REVELATION 22:17, 20

No couple preparing for a wedding, no student counting down to vacation, no traveler heading home ever awaited the future more eagerly than the author of Revelation, who ends his book—and the entire Bible—on a note of anticipation. Jesus is coming again in glory, and unbelievably wonderful things are coming down the road!

Amen! Come, Lord Jesus!

Acts 7:55–60
Psalm 97
Revelation 22:12–14, 16–17, 20
John 17:20–26

Monday
MAY 24

He said to them, "Did you receive the holy Spirit when you became believers?" They answered him, "We have never even heard that there is a holy Spirit."

—ACTS 19:2

Megan and Jeremy had been baptized and confirmed, but it wasn't until they attended a parish prayer-group meeting that they realized it was possible to have a personal relationship with the Holy Spirit.

"It is this Holy Spirit which will light in our hearts the flame of love. . . . How many know this Spirit of Love? And yet he alone is the source of their whole interior life" (Blessed Columba Marmion).

Acts 19:1–8
Psalm 68
John 16:29–33

Tuesday MAY 25

• SAINT BEDE THE VENERABLE, PRIEST AND DOCTOR OF THE CHURCH •
SAINT GREGORY VII, POPE • SAINT MARY MAGDALENE DE' PAZZI, VIRGIN •

Blessed be the Lord day by day,
God, our salvation, who carries us.
—PSALM 68:20

Our parents carry us for a time; then it's our turn to carry other little ones. From beginning to end, though, God holds both the carried and the carriers in the palm of his hand.

"Even to your old age I am the same,
even when your hair is gray I will bear you;
It is I who have done this, I who will continue,
and I who will carry you to safety" (Isaiah 46:4).

Acts 20:17–27
Psalm 68
John 17:1–11

Wednesday
MAY 26

• SAINT PHILIP NERI, PRIEST •

You know well that these very hands have served my needs and my companions. In every way I have shown you that by hard work of that sort we must help the weak, and keep in mind the words of the Lord Jesus who himself said, "It is more blessed to give than to receive."

—ACTS 20:34–35

In my area of town, there are immigrants from all over the world. I know that many of them regularly send part of their wages to the family members they had to leave behind.

What if I regularly sent part of my wages to some member of the human family who lives in a part of the world where work is harder to come by?

Acts 20:28–38
Psalm 68
John 17:11–19

Thursday MAY 27

• SAINT AUGUSTINE OF CANTERBURY, BISHOP •

I pray not only for them, but also for those who will believe in me through their word, so that they may all be one, as you, Father, are in me and I in you, that they also may be in us, that the world may believe that you sent me.

—JOHN 17:20–21

Are we so obviously united in love with God and with our brothers and sisters in Christ that the world stands back and says, "Hey, look at this!"?

Jesus, you know we're not there yet. Fill us with your love so that your prayer may be realized in us. Help your followers to become so united that we'll be like a neon sign pointing others to you.

Acts 22:30; 23:6–11
Psalm 16
John 17:20–26

Friday

MAY 28

When they had finished breakfast, Jesus said to Simon Peter, "Simon, son of John, do you love me more than these?" He said to him, "Yes, Lord, you know that I love you."

—JOHN 21:15

In his more foolish, self-reliant days, Peter might have taken the bait: "Yes, Lord, I certainly do love you more than all these others." The chastened Peter—the one to whom much had been forgiven—gave a simple answer grounded in self-knowledge.

When the Good Shepherd is looking to hire on a worker, he always wants to see humility and love on the résumé.

Acts 25:13–21
Psalm 103
John 21:15–19

Saturday
MAY 29

Peter turned and saw the disciple following whom Jesus loved. . . . When Peter saw him, he said to Jesus, "Lord, what about him?" Jesus said to him, . . . "What concern is it of yours? You follow me."

—JOHN 21:20–22

Ellen is so even-tempered. Is she like that at home?
"What concern is it of yours? You follow me."

Tom and Ann seem so much happier. They're not saying, but I bet something happened on that marriage retreat . . .
"What concern is it of yours? You follow me."

Lord, what happened between you and Joey at World Youth Day, anyway?
"What concern is it of yours? You follow me."

Acts 28:16–20, 30–31
Psalm 11
John 21:20–25

Sunday MAY 30

• PENTECOST SUNDAY •

There are different kinds of spiritual gifts but the same Spirit. . . . To each individual the manifestation of the Spirit is given for some benefit.

—1 CORINTHIANS 12:4, 7

What have I done with the gifts God has given me? Do I know what they are? Am I grateful for them, or do I long for other ones? Have I buried my gifts—out of laziness, fear of failure, or some other reason?

Holy Spirit, help me to take my place of service.

Vigil:

Genesis 11:1–9 or Exodus 19:3–8, 16–20 or Ezekiel 37:1–14 or Joel 3:1–5
Psalm 104
Romans 8:22–27
John 7:37–39

Day:

Acts 2:1–11
Psalm 104
1 Corinthians 12:3–7, 12–13 or Romans 8:8–17
John 20:19–23 or John 14:15–16, 23–26

Monday MAY 31

• THE VISITATION OF THE BLESSED VIRGIN MARY • MEMORIAL DAY •

With joy you will draw water
at the fountain of salvation.
—ISAIAH 12:3

In first-century Nazareth, drawing water was women's work. Mary probably began doing it as soon as she could hold a pitcher, accompanying her mother on daily runs to the village well to replenish the family water supply. Who could have known that one day Mary would be drinking from a limitless source of living water in her own home? Who could have known that she would channel that river of life to so many thirsting souls?

Zephaniah 3:14–18 or Romans 12:9–16
Isaiah 12:2–6
Luke 1:39–56

Tuesday JUNE 1

• SAINT JUSTIN, MARTYR •

They sent some Pharisees and Herodians to him to ensnare him in his speech. They came and said to him, "Teacher, we know that you are a truthful man and that you are not concerned with anyone's opinion. You do not regard a person's status but teach the way of God in accordance with the truth. Is it lawful to pay the census tax to Caesar or not?"

—MARK 12:13–14

They used true words to give a false impression. They spoke praise as the prelude to a trick question.

Utterly reprehensible! But so are my own attempts to manipulate the truth to fit my purposes.

2 Peter 3:12–15, 17–18
Psalm 90
Mark 12:13–17

Wednesday

JUNE 2

• SAINTS MARCELLINUS AND PETER, MARTYRS •

I know him in whom I have believed and am confident that he is able to guard what has been entrusted to me until that day.

—2 TIMOTHY 1:12

During the time that my father was practicing dentistry and I was one of his patients, it never occurred to me that drillings and fillings might be things to dread. I never worried, because I knew the patience and gentleness of the one who was safeguarding my teeth.

If I knew my Savior better, how much more secure I'd feel about entrusting every part of myself to his loving care.

2 Timothy 1:1–3, 6–12
Psalm 123
Mark 12:18–27

Thursday

JUNE 3

• SAINT CHARLES LWANGA AND COMPANIONS, MARTYRS •

You shall love your neighbor as yourself.

—MARK 12:31

Christ is the speaker in the following excerpt from St. Catherine of Siena's *Dialogue.* Try using it as a starting point for reflecting on today's verse:

"It is your duty to love your neighbors as your own self. In love you ought to help them spiritually with prayer and counsel, and assist them spiritually and materially in their need—at least with your good will if you have nothing else. If you do not love me, you do not love your neighbors. . . . But it is yourself you harm most, because you deprive yourself of grace."

2 Timothy 2:8–15
Psalm 25
Mark 12:28–34

Lovers of your teaching have much peace;
for them there is no stumbling block.
—PSALM 119:165

Peace? What about the cross? Persecution? The hard sayings of the gospel? What about Jesus' own admission that "in the world you will have trouble" (John 16:33)?

Maybe peace has less to do with a tranquil life than with the tranquillity of spirit that comes from absolute surrender and obedience to God.

2 Timothy 3:10–17
Psalm 119
Mark 12:35–37

Saturday JUNE 5

• SAINT BONIFACE, BISHOP AND MARTYR •

He sat down opposite the treasury and observed how the crowd put money into the treasury. Many rich people put in large sums. A poor widow also came and put in two small coins worth a few cents.

—MARK 12:41–42

He said he couldn't take being tied down anymore: "So many things I want to do before I die." But he wanted to have the children one weekend a month—for "quality time," when he would spend freely on treats and fun activities. On a tighter budget, she couldn't provide much more than the basics of love and faithfulness. She spent herself—and gave the children treasures that money can't buy.

2 Timothy 4:1–8
Psalm 71
Mark 12:38–44

Sunday JUNE 6

• THE MOST HOLY TRINITY •

[T]he love of God has been poured out into our hearts through the holy Spirit that has been given to us.

—ROMANS 5:5

Just when you're feeling like an eroded, overfarmed field in a drought, along comes the Holy Spirit to open the floodgates and lay down new irrigation channels for God's love to flow through.

Proverbs 8:22–31
Psalm 8
Romans 5:1–5
John 16:12–15

Monday JUNE 7

Blessed are the poor in spirit,
for theirs is the kingdom of heaven.
—MATTHEW 5:3

One evening as he prayed before the Blessed Sacrament, Brendan received the grace to stop pretending and to admit his spiritual poverty. "Lord, what am I going to do with my life? Where am I going? I've been on automatic pilot lately—but I really don't have a clue what your plan is, or even what will make me happy. Please help me, Lord."

Brendan didn't walk away with any specific answers that evening. But he did feel somehow closer to the kingdom of heaven.

1 Kings 17:1–6
Psalm 121
Matthew 5:1–12

Tuesday JUNE 8

[Y]our light must shine before others, that they may see your good deeds and glorify your heavenly Father.

—MATTHEW 5:16

Doing the good deeds is only the first part of the task. The greater challenge is doing them in a way that draws attention to God's goodness, not our own.

How are we going to do that?

1 Kings 17:7–16
Psalm 4
Matthew 5:13–16

Wednesday

JUNE 9

• SAINT EPHREM, DEACON AND DOCTOR OF THE CHURCH •

Taking the young bull that was turned over to them, [the prophets of Baal] prepared it and called on Baal from morning to noon, saying, "Answer us, Baal!" But there was no sound, and no one answering. And they hopped around the altar they had prepared. When it was noon, Elijah taunted them: "Call louder, for he is a god and may be meditating, or may have retired, or may be on a journey. Perhaps he is asleep and must be awakened."

—1 KINGS 18:26–27

Sometimes all it takes to keep us focused on the truth is a healthy sense of the ridiculous.

1 Kings 18:20–39
Psalm 16
Matthew 5:17–19

Thursday

JUNE 10

But I say to you, whoever is angry with his brother will be liable to judgment, and whoever says to his brother, "Raqa," will be answerable to the Sanhedrin, and whoever says, "You fool," will be liable to fiery Gehenna.

—MATTHEW 5:22

James has the idea that Christians aren't ever supposed to feel or express anger. As he discovers that he can't root it out of himself, his failure makes him even angrier.

Jackie is working on redirecting her anger so that it targets the things that make God angry. She's starting with her old scornful way of putting people down with demeaning, hurtful remarks and epithets like *dummy, ignoramus,* and *stupid.* She's making real progress.

1 Kings 18:41–46
Psalm 65
Matthew 5:20–26

Friday

JUNE 11

• SAINT BARNABAS, APOSTLE •

[T]hey sent Barnabas [to go] to Antioch. When he arrived and saw the grace of God, he rejoiced and encouraged them all to remain faithful to the Lord in firmness of heart.

—ACTS 11:22–23

God is doing such great things in their lives!
(But what about mine?)

So many new people are coming to their church services!
(Why is my parish so dead?)

Those people really know how to love one another!
(How come nobody knows how to love me?)

When the poisonous voice of envy begins to whisper in our ears, brother Barnabas, pray for us.

Acts 11:21–26; 13:1–3
Psalm 98
Matthew 5:27–32

Saturday

JUNE 12

I keep the LORD always before me;
with the Lord at my right, I shall never be shaken.

—PSALM 16:8

Imagine your mind as a computer desktop. What's on it? What's the wallpaper? The screen saver? And do you have the most important icon prominently displayed?

1 Kings 19:19–21
Psalm 16
Matthew 5:33–37

• THE MOST HOLY BODY AND BLOOD OF CHRIST •

Then taking the five loaves and the two fish, and looking up to heaven, he said the blessing over them, broke them, and gave them to the disciples to set before the crowd. They all ate and were satisfied.

—LUKE 9:16–17

Jesus, you satisfy our hungry hearts by nourishing us with your own body and blood. May your sacrifice strengthen us to lay down our lives so that others may be satisfied too.

Genesis 14:18–20
Psalm 110
1 Corinthians 11:23–26
Luke 9:11–17

When someone strikes you on [your] right cheek, turn the other one to him as well. If anyone wants to go to law with you over your tunic, hand him your cloak as well. Should anyone press you into service for one mile, go with him for two miles.

—MATTHEW 5:39–41

When your spouse is out of sorts, fight your own grouchiness and find little ways to show your love . . . When your teenager needs to talk, make an extra effort to listen attentively—even if it's two in the morning . . . When a lonely relative asks you to pick up a few items at the supermarket, stay and visit when you make the delivery . . . When your sister asks to borrow your favorite dress, offer your favorite necklace as well . . .

1 Kings 21:1–16
Psalm 5
Matthew 5:38–42

Tuesday

JUNE 15

Wash away all my guilt;
from my sin cleanse me.
—PSALM 51:4

Every spring, my Aunt Mary would declare a war on dirt. She would enlist my less bellicose Aunt Leone in the campaign, and they would advance inexorably through the house, reclaiming territory from room to room. The kitchen ceiling was repainted, every dish was washed, attic and cellar floors were scrubbed—no germ escaped. When the whole house gleamed, my tired but triumphant aunts would put away their weapons and enjoy a cup of tea.

Mary's spring-cleaning battle plan gets me thinking about the drastic measures that might be needed to purify my inner house.

1 Kings 21:17–29
Psalm 51
Matthew 5:43–48

Wednesday

JUNE 16

When you pray, do not be like the hypocrites, who love to stand and pray in the synagogues and on street corners so that others may see them. Amen, I say to you, they have received their reward. But when you pray, go to your inner room, close the door, and pray to your Father in secret. And your Father who sees in secret will repay you.

—MATTHEW 6:5–6

She never prayed in an ostentatious way when she was at church or in the adoration chapel. But she did derive some satisfaction from watching herself at prayer in her mind's eye. It reinforced her secret feeling that she was sort of holy.

2 Kings 2:1, 6–14
Psalm 31
Matthew 6:1–6, 16–18

Thursday JUNE 17

This is how you are to pray:
Our Father in heaven,
hallowed be your name . . .
—MATTHEW 6:9

When we say the Our Father, we come to God in trust and love, in longing, adoration, thanks, praise, and every basic attitude of prayer—all simply and beautifully strung together, like pearls on a necklace. Each pearl can be worn singly too. Choose one for today, and let it lead you into brief but frequent praying from the heart.

Sirach 48:1–14
Psalm 97
Matthew 6:7–15

Friday

JUNE 18

• THE MOST SACRED HEART OF JESUS •

Only goodness and love will pursue me
all the days of my life;
I will dwell in the house of the LORD
for years to come.
—PSALM 23:6

My husband tells me that the Hebrew word here translated "pursue" is very vigorous and means "hunt" or "chase." Which leads to speculation: Is the psalmist being playful? Will we be hunted down by God's goodness and love? Or perhaps we are to think of a pair of hunting dogs named Goodness and Love that greet us when we arrive at the Lord's house for dinner!

Ezekiel 34:11–16
Psalm 23
Romans 5:5–11
Luke 15:3–7

• THE IMMACULATE HEART OF MARY •

[H]is mother kept all these things in her heart.

—LUKE 2:51

Often before she does a quilting project, my mother sets out the various pieces of fabric she's planning to use. She lives with them for a time until patterns and color combinations suggest themselves. Then she's ready to begin.

The way I see it, Mom's way of quilting has something in common with Mary's way of pondering.

2 Chronicles 24:17–25
Psalm 89
Luke 2:41–51

Sunday JUNE 20

• FATHER'S DAY •

He said, "The Son of Man must suffer greatly and be rejected by the elders, the chief priests, and the scribes, and be killed and on the third day be raised."

—LUKE 9:22

While on a business trip to Montreal, I took a walk that led me through a large cemetery. Reading the gravestone inscriptions, so evocative of loss and sorrow and dreams unfulfilled, I felt the shadow of the cross. But a family marker shaped like an obelisk stopped me in my tracks. In boldly chiseled letters, it listed the names of deceased family members, beneath a simple declaration of faith: *Here, awaiting the resurrection of the dead, lie . . .* It was a beam of resurrection light.

Zechariah 12:10–11; 13:1
Psalm 62
Galatians 3:26–29
Luke 9:18–24

Monday

JUNE 21

• SAINT ALOYSIUS GONZAGA, RELIGIOUS •

Why do you notice the splinter in your brother's eye, but do not perceive the wooden beam in your own eye? How can you say to your brother, "Let me remove that splinter from your eye," while the wooden beam is in your eye? You hypocrite, remove the wooden beam from your eye first; then you will see clearly to remove the splinter from your brother's eye.

—MATTHEW 7:3–5

The sins and weaknesses that bother us the most when we see them in others are usually the very ones that are most destructive in us. If we get help for our own beams and splinters, we can provide genuine, experiential help to others. If we don't, we'll just go around blind and blinding.

2 Kings 17:5–8, 13–15, 18
Psalm 60
Matthew 7:1–5

Tuesday

JUNE 22

• SAINT PAULINUS OF NOLA, BISHOP • SAINT JOHN FISHER, BISHOP AND MARTYR • SAINT THOMAS MORE, MARTYR •

Enter through the narrow gate; for the gate is wide and the road broad that leads to destruction, and those who enter through it are many. How narrow the gate and constricted the road that leads to life. And those who find it are few.

—MATTHEW 7:13–14

How crowded the mall with its abundance of chain stores full of trendy luxury goods, and how easy it is to shop there. How small the little out-of-the-way shop offering simple, timeless basics, and how few ever think to search it out.

Am I following the crowds to the megamall of the world? Do I even know where that little shop is?

2 Kings 19:9–11, 14–21, 31–36
Psalm 48
Matthew 7:6, 12–14

Wednesday

JUNE 23

The king went up to the temple of the LORD with all the men of Judah and all the inhabitants of Jerusalem: priests, prophets, and all the people, small and great. . . . Standing by the column, the king made a covenant before the LORD that they would follow him and observe his ordinances, statutes and decrees with their whole hearts and souls. . . . And all the people stood as participants in the covenant.

—2 KINGS 23:2–3

When she returned to the church after a long time away, Lisa decided to go on a weeklong retreat. It was an expression of her desire to reclaim every part of herself and present it to God, to proclaim her allegiance with every fiber of her being.

2 Kings 22:8–13; 23:1–3
Psalm 119
Matthew 7:15–20

Thursday

JUNE 24

• THE NATIVITY OF SAINT JOHN THE BAPTIST •

[A]s John was completing his course, he would say, "What do you suppose that I am? I am not he. Behold, one is coming after me; I am not worthy to unfasten the sandals of his feet."

—ACTS 13:25

"Among those born of women, no one is greater than John," Jesus said (Luke 7:28). The proof? When the truly great One came along, John singled him out and was only too eager to fade into the woodwork.

Vigil:
Jeremiah 1:4–10
Psalm 71
1 Peter 1:8–12
Luke 1:5–17

Day:
Isaiah 49:1–6
Psalm 139
Acts 13:22–26
Luke 1:57–66, 80

Friday

JUNE 25

By the rivers of Babylon
we sat mourning and weeping
when we remembered Zion.
—PSALM 137:1

Our world is full of people longing for home—exiles, homesick students and travelers, displaced populations, prisoners, migrant workers, nursing-home residents, hospital patients.

We can pray for them with a sense of solidarity. After all, even the most rooted among us are pilgrims awaiting entrance into our heavenly homeland.

2 Kings 25:1–12
Psalm 137
Matthew 8:1–4

Saturday

JUNE 26

Rise up, shrill in the night,
at the beginning of every watch;
Pour out your heart like water
in the presence of the Lord.
—LAMENTATIONS 2:19

Joan usually prayed to find solace, calm, and peace for herself and her family. But the newspaper accounts of how people were suffering in the Middle East so disturbed her that she began interceding for them, letting tears and sorrow enter freely into her prayers.

In a world where famine, war, enslavement, disease, unemployment, poverty, and gross injustice are facts of life for millions, we sometimes need to pray with feeling—even if we live in a more or less tranquil spot.

Lamentations 2:2, 10–14, 18–19
Psalm 74
Matthew 8:5–17

Sunday

JUNE 27

Jesus said, "No one who sets a hand to the plow and looks to what was left behind is fit for the kingdom of God."

—LUKE 9:62

If you left your heart in San Francisco, how will you be able to carry on with your life when you move to Dubuque?

1 Kings 19:16, 19–21
Psalm 16
Galatians 5:1, 13–18
Luke 9:51–62

Monday

JUNE 28

• SAINT IRENAEUS, BISHOP AND MARTYR •

[T]hey sell the just man for silver,
and the poor man for a pair of sandals.
They trample the heads of the weak
into the dust of the earth,
and force the lowly out of the way.

—AMOS 2:6–7

I'm not oppressing anyone! I don't run a sweatshop or a factory where ten year olds spend fourteen hours a day making running shoes. And I don't know anyone who does. I don't know any of the oppressed either. Those people are all far away—off in the Pacific Rim or somewhere.

So why do I feel their needs so near in the voices of ancient prophets? Will I choose to listen? Will I choose to care? Will I choose to act?

Amos 2:6–10, 13–16
Psalm 50
Matthew 8:18–22

Tuesday

JUNE 29

• SAINTS PETER AND PAUL, APOSTLES •

I have competed well; I have finished the race; I have kept the faith. From now on the crown of righteousness awaits me, which the Lord, the just judge, will award to me on that day, and not only to me, but to all who have longed for his appearance.

—2 TIMOTHY 4:7–8

Our service to God is important. At the end of our lives, though, what will matter most is whether our gravestones and obituary notices can truthfully proclaim that we stayed close to Christ till the end, that we "kept the faith."

Lord, grant us and those we love the grace of final perseverance.

Vigil:
Acts 3:1–10
Psalm 19
Galatians 1:11–20
John 21:15–19

Day:
Acts 12:1–11
Psalm 34
2 Timothy 4:6–8, 17–18
Matthew 16:13–19

Wednesday

JUNE 30

• THE FIRST HOLY MARTYRS OF THE HOLY ROMAN CHURCH •

Some distance away a herd of many swine was feeding. The demons pleaded with him, "If you drive us out, send us into the herd of swine." And he said to them, "Go then!" They came out and entered the swine, and the whole herd rushed down the steep bank into the sea where they drowned.

—MATTHEW 8:30–32

Could there possibly be a more obvious illustration of the Evil One's destructive intentions for God's creation? For me?

Amos 5:14–15, 21–24
Psalm 50
Matthew 8:28–34

The law of the LORD is perfect,
refreshing the soul. . . .
The precepts of the LORD are right,
rejoicing the heart.
—PSALM 19:8–9

He was a second grader—too young to analyze exactly why he liked Miss Roy's class so much better than Mr. White's. Years later, he understood. She'd had a few basic rules. There was order. Kids could learn. He'd felt safe.

For adults too, the right ground rules make for the best learning conditions.

Amos 7:10–17
Psalm 19
Matthew 9:1–8

Friday

JULY 2

While he was at table in his house, many tax collectors and sinners came and sat with Jesus and his disciples. The Pharisees saw this and said to his disciples, "Why does your teacher eat with tax collectors and sinners?"

—MATTHEW 9:10–11

The Pharisees could have directed their question to Jesus himself. Perhaps they chose not to because they feared losing an argument in public—which is exactly what happened when Jesus overheard their question (Matthew 9:12–13).

The lessons for us? First, the voice of doubt always addresses the weakest link. And second, all insidious questions should be referred to Jesus.

Amos 8:4–6, 9–12
Psalm 119
Matthew 9:9–13

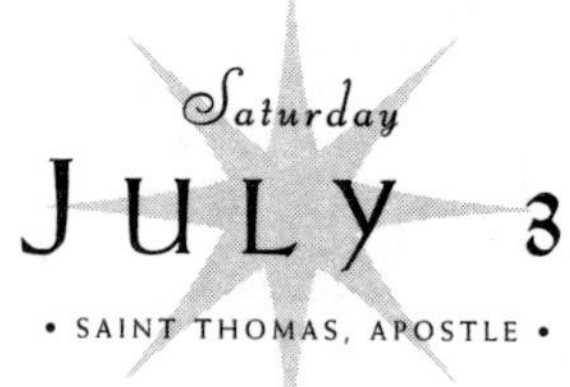

Saturday JULY 3

• SAINT THOMAS, APOSTLE •

So then you are no longer strangers and sojourners, but you are fellow citizens with the holy ones and members of the household of God.

—EPHESIANS 2:19

Someday we'll know the joy of walking into God's house and making the same announcement we now use to broadcast our return from work or school or shopping trips: "I'm home!"

Of course, as God's children, we're already home. It's just that our section of the house doesn't always reflect its Owner as well as the upper level does.

Ephesians 2:19–22
Psalm 117
John 20:24–29

[Y]our heart shall rejoice,
and your bodies flourish like the grass;
The LORD's power shall be known to his servants.
—ISAIAH 66:14

Flourish like grass? To the average suburbanite, who wishes the lawn wouldn't need such frequent mowing, this doesn't sound like such a great promise. It's the desert dweller who gets the picture: barren sands bursting into bloom when the rains come.

Lord, when your power is poured out, even dry bones will spring suddenly to life!

Isaiah 66:10–14
Psalm 66
Galatians 6:14–18
Luke 10:1–12, 17–20 or 10:1–9

Monday

JULY 5

• SAINT ANTHONY MARY ZACCARIA, PRIEST •

A woman suffering hemorrhages for twelve years came up behind him and touched the tassel on his cloak. . . . Jesus turned around and saw her, and said, "Courage, daughter! Your faith has saved you."

—MATTHEW 9:20, 22

Once, in a foreign country, I accompanied a friend to an eye surgeon's office. After undergoing numerous indignities, my friend was ushered in before the surgeon, who disdainfully ignored his questions and seemed to demand worship. "I feel like the woman who suffered much at the hands of many physicians," my friend groaned later, alluding to Luke's version of the story (8:43).

Great Physician, I want to be like you. Teach me to approach people who suffer in a way that affirms their dignity and imparts courage.

Hosea 2:16–18, 21–22
Psalm 145
Matthew 9:18–26

Tuesday JULY 6

• SAINT MARIA GORETTI, VIRGIN AND MARTYR •

With their silver and gold they made
idols for themselves, to their own destruction.
—HOSEA 8:4

They made good grades so that they could make good money and pursue the good life. They built fantasy worlds where they could forget about everything but having fun. They created entire industries characterized by manipulation and self-promotion. They squandered their minds and skills on selfish, shallow pursuits. So many God-given raw materials gone to waste, or worse.

Hosea 8:4–7, 11–13
Psalm 115
Matthew 9:32–38

Wednesday

JULY 7

As you go, make this proclamation: "The kingdom of heaven is at hand."

—MATTHEW 10:7

Make it as you walk into your next meeting, as you head down the canned-goods aisle in the supermarket, as you drive to your brother-in-law's to watch the football game. Even if you don't use words, reflect God's kingdom in those in-between moments, "as you go."

Hosea 10:1–3, 7–8, 12
Psalm 105
Matthew 10:1–7

Thursday

JULY 8

I drew them with human cords,
with bands of love. . . .
Yet, though I stooped to feed my child,
they did not know that I was their healer.
—HOSEA 11:4

The night I felt so depressed and just happened to run into someone I could talk to . . . Did you arrange that, Lord?

The unexpected burst of courage that allowed me to speak up at that meeting . . . Was that your doing, Lord?

The way the right house turned up exactly when we needed a place to live . . . You did that too, didn't you?

You've always been so close, Lord. I see it now. Thank you!

Hosea 11:1–4, 8–9
Psalm 80
Matthew 10:7–15

Friday JULY 9

• SAINT AUGUSTINE ZHAO RONG, PRIEST, AND HIS COMPANIONS, CHINESE MARTYRS •

[B]e shrewd as serpents and simple as doves.

—MATTHEW 10:16

If we're shrewd, we'll choose our battles wisely, assess the costs accurately, and pay the price to safeguard our resources. If we're simple, we'll refuse to retaliate against those who draw us into battle. Wisdom and innocence—we need both as our comrades-in-arms.

Hosea 14:2–10
Psalm 51
Matthew 10:16–23

Saturday

JULY 10

"Holy, holy, holy is the LORD of hosts! . . . All the earth is filled with his glory!" At the sound of that cry, the frame of the door shook and the house was filled with smoke.

Then I said, "Woe is me, I am doomed! For I am a man of unclean lips, living among a people of unclean lips; yet my eyes have seen the King, the LORD of hosts!"

—ISAIAH 6:3–5

Lord God, light of lights, we can no more bear a tiny ray of your glory than we can stare into the sun! Even a single photon of your radiance would blind us! Reveal to us as much of yourself as we can bear. Burn our sins away so that we can come into your presence and see your face.

Isaiah 6:1–8
Psalm 93
Matthew 10:24–33

Sunday

July 11

Jesus replied, "A man fell victim to robbers as he went down from Jerusalem to Jericho. They stripped and beat him and went off leaving him half-dead. A priest happened to be going down that road, but when he saw him, he passed by on the opposite side. Likewise a Levite came to the place, and when he saw him, he passed by on the opposite side. But a Samaritan traveler who came upon him was moved with compassion at the sight."

—Luke 10:30–33

The first two travelers who happened on the crime scene were concerned about their schedules, their ritual purity, their safety. They were preoccupied with *What will happen to me?* The Samaritan had the compassion to wonder, *What will happen to him?*

Deuteronomy 30:10–14
Psalm 69
Colossians 1:15–20
Luke 10:25–37

Monday JULY 12

When you spread out your hands,
I close my eyes to you. . . .
I will not listen.
Your hands are full of blood!
—ISAIAH 1:15

A police officer recently went to court wearing the distinctive twelve-hundred-dollar designer glasses that had disappeared during the drug raid he had helped to conduct. The defendant's wife recognized the stolen goods, and now it's the officer who's on trial.

A dumb move? Yes, but no dumber than coming to prayer displaying the stains of unrepented sins. However we try to conceal them, they are visible to the Lord, who wants to help us be "clean of hand and pure of heart" (Psalm 24:4).

Isaiah 1:10–17
Psalm 50
Matthew 10:34–11:1

Tuesday JULY 13

• SAINT HENRY •

Unless your faith is firm
you shall not be firm!
—ISAIAH 7:9

The Christian life is like a suspension bridge with its thousands of vehicles traveling high above the river on ribbons of concrete.

What holds the whole thing up? What keeps it from collapse? Only a fine tracery of steel cable, the invisible support of faith in God. Every Christian life depends on that.

Isaiah 7:1–9
Psalm 48
Matthew 11:20–24

Wednesday

JULY 14

• BLESSED KATERI TEKAKWITHA, VIRGIN •

At that time Jesus said in reply, "I give praise to you, Father, Lord of heaven and earth, for although you have hidden these things from the wise and the learned you have revealed them to the childlike."

—MATTHEW 11:25

Baby Stephen looks out on the world with big blue eyes, eagerly taking everything in, locking eyes with anyone who looks his way. With few preconceived notions about who he is and what's out there, his whole being is aquiver with the excitement of discovery. He's a tiny explorer setting out to find new worlds by feeling, seeing, sniffing, tasting, and experimenting with sounds and movements and processes.

Those of us seeking to explore God's kingdom could take a lesson from baby Stephen and cultivate receptivity.

Isaiah 10:5–7, 13–16
Psalm 94
Matthew 11:25–27

Thursday

JULY 15

• SAINT BONAVENTURE, BISHOP AND DOCTOR OF THE CHURCH •

Take my yoke upon you and learn from me. . . . For my yoke is easy, and my burden light.

—MATTHEW 11:29–30

Every demanding discipline is made easier by a teacher who not only shows us the right path but who walks with us every step of the way.

Isaiah 26:7–9, 12, 16–19
Psalm 102
Matthew 11:28–30

Friday

JULY 16

• OUR LADY OF MOUNT CARMEL •

I said, "I shall see the LORD no more
in the land of the living.
No longer shall I behold my fellow men
among those who dwell in the world."
—ISAIAH 38:11

Help me, Lord, to face the fact that I will die one day. Today I offer you my life. Enable me to live it well so that I may die well and know the joy of beholding you for all eternity.

Holy Mary, mother of God,
pray for us sinners
now and at the hour of our death.

Isaiah 38:1–6, 21–22, 7–8
Isaiah 38:10–12, 16
Matthew 12:1–8

Saturday JULY 17

Woe to those who plan iniquity,
and work out evil on their couches;
In the morning light they accomplish it
when it lies within their power.

—MICAH 2:1

Once, just because I was miffed at having been left out of the loop, I tricked a friend into divulging a piece of news. It was an item of no consequence, and my friend never picked up on the ruse. Yet because my action was deliberate, I felt more shocked and shamefaced than if I had acted out of momentary weakness or inattention. Suddenly revealed to myself, I understood more clearly why I will always need a Savior.

Micah 2:1–5
Psalm 10
Matthew 12:14–21

Sunday

JULY 18

Martha, burdened with much serving, came to him and said, "Lord, do you not care that my sister has left me by myself to do the serving? Tell her to help me." The Lord said to her in reply, "Martha, Martha, you are anxious and worried about many things. There is need of only one thing. Mary has chosen the better part and it will not be taken from her."

—LUKE 10:40–42

Lord, don't you care about our cares—about all those things that trouble, anger, and upset us? Or is it that you care about us too much to let us get by with wanting less than the best?

Jesus, teach us to see our cares in light of what *you* care about.

Genesis 18:1–10
Psalm 15
Colossians 1:24–28
Luke 10:38–42

Monday
July 19

Those who offer praise as a sacrifice honor me.

—Psalm 50:23

Every day, all over the world, the whole of creation loved by God is presented to the Father through the death and resurrection of Christ. In magnificent cathedrals and airport chapels, in mission churches and auditoriums, in monasteries and prison cells, the church in union with its great High Priest gives thanks for all that God has made good, beautiful, and just in creation and in humanity. The Mass is the perfect sacrifice of praise, the perfect response to Psalm 50, verse 23.

Micah 6:1–4, 6–8
Psalm 50
Matthew 12:38–42

July 20

• SAINT APOLLINARIUS, BISHOP AND MARTYR •

And stretching out his hand toward his disciples, he said, "Here are my mother and my brothers. For whoever does the will of my heavenly Father is my brother, and sister, and mother."

—MATTHEW 12:49–50

You were not born too late. Even now as you read these verses, Jesus is stretching out his hand, inviting you into the family circle of people closest to him. Your place is reserved. Why not claim it today, by renewing your resolve to do your Father's will?

Micah 7:14–15, 18–20
Psalm 85
Matthew 12:46–50

Wednesday

JULY 21

• SAINT LAWRENCE OF BRINDISI, PRIEST AND DOCTOR OF THE CHURCH •

"Ah, Lord GOD!" I said,
"I know not how to speak; I am too young."
But the LORD answered me,
Say not, "I am too young."
—JEREMIAH 1:6–7

Say not, "I am too old" either. And while you're at it, you can also stop using excuses like "I'm too embarrassed . . . too uneducated . . . not good with people . . . not the right type." When God calls you to do something, set aside every fearful excuse and move ahead with a confident "Here I am."

Jeremiah 1:1, 4–10
Psalm 71
Matthew 13:1–9

Thursday JULY 22

• SAINT MARY MAGDALENE •

Two evils have my people done:
they have forsaken me, the source of living waters;
They have dug themselves cisterns,
broken cisterns, that hold no water.

—JEREMIAH 2:13

In ancient times, people who had the good fortune to live near rivers and streams had no reason to undertake the arduous work of digging pits to store rainwater. Besides, who would have chosen to drink stagnant water when they could dip their pitchers into flowing streams?

And why do we try to quench our thirst for happiness anywhere but at the fountain of living water that Jesus offers? It makes just as little sense.

Jeremiah 2:1–3, 7–8, 12–13
Psalm 63
John 20:1–2, 11–18

Friday

JULY 23

• SAINT BRIDGET OF SWEDEN, RELIGIOUS •

But the seed sown on rich soil is the one who hears the word and understands it, who indeed bears fruit and yields a hundred or sixty or thirtyfold.

—MATTHEW 13:23

The success of the flower seeds I plant depends on whether I've paid attention to things like frost zones, germination times, and shade and sunlight patterns.

The seeds that God scatters are more robust. In season and out, no matter what the planting conditions, they inevitably produce the highest yield in every soil type that welcomes them.

Jeremiah 3:14–17
Jeremiah 31:10–13
Matthew 13:18–23

Saturday JULY 24

• SAINT SHARBEL MAKHLUF, PRIEST •

[I]f you pull up the weeds you might uproot the wheat along with them. Let them grow together until harvest; then at harvest time I will say to the harvesters, "First collect the weeds and tie them in bundles for burning; but gather the wheat into my barn."

—MATTHEW 13:29–30

Joseph Stalin was an altar boy. Judas started out as a seemingly committed disciple. Not so promising in their early years were Zacchaeus, St. Augustine, and Dorothy Day. What looks like a weed at the moment may turn out to be the finest wheat come harvest time.

Jeremiah 7:1–11
Psalm 84
Matthew 13:24–30

Sunday
JULY 25

And I tell you, ask and you will receive; seek and you will find; knock and the door will be opened to you. For everyone who asks, receives; and the one who seeks, finds; and to the one who knocks, the door will be opened.

—LUKE 11:9–10

Ask with the persistence of the telemarketer! Seek with the doggedness of the bill collector or the nosy relative who comes to snoop around for information! Knock with the determination of the door-to-door proselytizer or the Girl Scout trying to make her cookie-sales quota! It's okay to be pushy. God won't be put off.

Genesis 18:20–32
Psalm 138
Colossians 2:12–14
Luke 11:1–13

Monday

JULY 26

• SAINTS JOACHIM AND ANNE, PARENTS OF THE BLESSED VIRGIN MARY •

The kingdom of heaven is like a mustard seed that a person took and sowed in a field. It is the smallest of all the seeds, yet when full-grown it is the largest of plants. It becomes a large bush, and the "birds of the sky come and dwell in its branches."

—MATTHEW 13:31–32

Jenny couldn't quite bring herself to say she believed in God, but one evening, as she sat on the porch steps smoking a cigarette and admiring the sunset, she had the inspiration to pray, "God, if you exist, show me." Years later, she marveled at how that little seed had taken root and grown. It had become a source of strength and blessing not only for Jenny but also for everyone in her life.

Jeremiah 13:1–11
Deuteronomy 32:18–21
Matthew 13:31–35

Tuesday JULY 27

Help us, God our savior,
for the glory of your name.
Deliver us, pardon our sins
for your name's sake.
Why should the nations say,
"Where is their God?"
—PSALM 79:9–10

Because of my sins, I have all too much in common with those obnoxious loudmouths who inevitably embarrass their relatives in social situations. Lord, I don't want to be an embarrassment to you and your family. Please—for *your* sake—make me holy as you are holy. Help me to become a fitting and effective witness to you.

Jeremiah 14:17–22
Psalm 79
Matthew 13:36–43

Wednesday
JULY 28

When I found your words, I devoured them;
they became my joy and the happiness of my heart.
—JEREMIAH 15:16

People devour all sorts of words—sports pages, romance novels, stock-market reports, comic strips, whodunits, online smut and silliness. Perhaps we'd be more discriminating if we realized that the old adage "You are what you eat" holds true not only for the body but also for the mind and soul.

Jeremiah 15:10, 16–21
Psalm 59
Matthew 13:44–46

Jesus told her, "I am the resurrection and the life; whoever believes in me, even if he dies, will live, and everyone who lives and believes in me will never die. Do you believe this?" She said to him, "Yes, Lord. I have come to believe that you are the Messiah, the Son of God, the one who is coming into the world."

—JOHN 11:25–27

Lord, today I will make Martha's prayer my own. And even if I don't see in my earthly life what she saw in hers—a human corpse brought back to life at your command—I do firmly believe that I will see it on the last day.

Jeremiah 18:1–6
Psalm 146
John 11:19–27 or Luke 10:38–42

Friday July 30

• SAINT PETER CHRYSOLOGUS, BISHOP AND DOCTOR OF THE CHURCH •

Now the priests, the prophets, and all the people heard Jeremiah speak these words in the house of the LORD. When Jeremiah finished speaking all that the LORD bade him speak to all the people, the priests and prophets laid hold of him, crying, "You must be put to death!"

—JEREMIAH 26:7–8

When the voice of conscience speaks some unwelcome word to our inner hearts, give us the grace to receive it with humility rather than stifling it with angry shouts.

Jeremiah 26:1–9
Psalm 69
Matthew 13:54–58

Saturday JULY 31

• SAINT IGNATIUS OF LOYOLA, PRIEST •

At that time Herod the tetrarch heard of the reputation of Jesus and said to his servants, "This man is John the Baptist. He has been raised from the dead; that is why mighty powers are at work in him."

—MATTHEW 14:1–2

Herod couldn't be bothered with correcting his muddled ideas. He found Jesus and John mildly curious and puzzling but hardly worthy of an ambitious leader's time and attention. Herod was too intent on his big career plans to take notice of the *really* big plans that God was carrying out right before his eyes.

Whenever we pursue our lives and goals in a way that makes us oblivious to what God is doing in the world around us, we exhibit the blindness of Herod.

Jeremiah 26:11–16, 24
Psalm 69
Matthew 14:1–12

Sunday

AUGUST 1

Then he said to the crowd, "Take care to guard against all greed."
—LUKE 12:15

Greed grasps at whatever it thinks will bring security and stockpiles it "just in case." It excels in excess and longs to corner the market on everything it deems valuable. Greed never stops trying to fill its closets and freezers, its garages, portfolios, libraries, information banks, and whatever else can house its special treasures. Greed is like a restless, unpleasant spouse who is perpetually dissatisfied with the family's standard of living.

Ecclesiastes 1:2; 2:21–23
Psalm 95
Colossians 3:1–5, 9–11
Luke 12:13–21

Monday

AUGUST 2

• SAINT EUSEBIUS OF VERCELLI, BISHOP • SAINT PETER JULIAN EYMARD, PRIEST •

[T]he prophet who prophesies peace is recognized as truly sent by the LORD only when his prophetic prediction is fulfilled.

—JEREMIAH 28:9

Until a routine test revealed it during her first pregnancy, Missy and her husband didn't know they were both carriers for sickle cell anemia. Some well-meaning friends told them not to worry, that their baby would be okay. Wiser ones prayed, refrained from offering false hope, and found practical ways to express love and support. Those were the friends Missy sought out after the baby was born.

Jeremiah 28:1–17
Psalm 119
Matthew 14:13–21

Tuesday

AUGUST 3

At once [Jesus] spoke to them, "Take courage, it is I; do not be afraid." Peter said to him in reply, "Lord, if it is you, command me to come to you on the water." He said, "Come." Peter got out of the boat and began to walk on the water toward Jesus.

—MATTHEW 14:27–29

Given the circumstances—a *Perfect Storm* setting of strong winds and rough water—the identity test that Peter came up with isn't the one that I would have devised. "Lord, if it is you, command the wind and waves to die down" would probably have been my choice.

Peter didn't sail through his test with flying colors, but he was willing to identify a risky step of faith and take it. Am I that gutsy?

Jeremiah 30:1–2, 12–15, 18–22
Psalm 102
Matthew 14:22–36 or Matthew 15:1–2, 10–14

Wednesday

AUGUST 4

• SAINT JOHN MARY VIANNEY, PRIEST •

With age-old love I have loved you;
so I have kept my mercy toward you.
Again I will restore you, and you shall be rebuilt,
O virgin Israel;
Carrying your festive tambourines,
you shall go forth dancing with the merrymakers.
—JEREMIAH 31:3–4

In your kingdom, your people will crowd onto the celestial dance floor in celebration of your faithful love. But even now, we catch echoes of the festive tambourines! Our hearts leap up, our spirits move in step with heaven's great triumphal dance.

Jeremiah 31:1–7
Jeremiah 31:10–13
Matthew 15:21–28

Thursday

AUGUST 5

• THE DEDICATION OF THE BASILICA OF SAINT MARY MAJOR IN ROME •

From that time on, Jesus began to show his disciples that he must go to Jerusalem and suffer greatly from the elders, the chief priests, and the scribes, and be killed and on the third day be raised. Then Peter took him aside and began to rebuke him, "God forbid, Lord! No such thing shall ever happen to you." He turned and said to Peter, "Get behind me, Satan! You are an obstacle to me. You are thinking not as God does, but as human beings do."

—MATTHEW 16:21–23

Lord, help me to get behind you and to get with your program—even when your wisdom strikes me as folly.

Jeremiah 31:31–34
Psalm 51
Matthew 16:13–23

Friday

AUGUST 6

• THE TRANSFIGURATION OF THE LORD •

While [Jesus] was praying his face changed in appearance and his clothing became dazzling white. . . . Peter and his companions had been overcome by sleep, but becoming fully awake, they saw his glory.

—LUKE 9:29, 32

An Irishman was walking into a study hall one ordinary day when he received a sudden profound revelation, a "light on the infinity of God." The experience reshaped his life and made him the man we now venerate as Blessed Columba Marmion, Benedictine abbot and spiritual counselor.

Flashes of God's glory shining into our ordinary surroundings—little transfigurations that God offers to anyone who is "fully awake" to their transforming potential.

Daniel 7:9–10, 13–14
Psalm 97
2 Peter 1:16–19
Luke 9:28–36

Saturday

AUGUST 7

• SAINT SIXTUS II, POPE AND MARTYR, AND HIS COMPANIONS, MARTYRS •
SAINT CAJETAN, PRIEST •

I will stand at my guard post,
and station myself upon the rampart,
And keep watch to see what he will say to me,
and what answer he will give to my complaint.

—HABAKKUK 2:1

It's never a matter of *whether* you will speak to us, but of what you will say, and when. It's the certainty of your coming that keeps us at our posts of prayer, on eager lookout for every sign of your presence.

Habakkuk 1:12–2:4
Psalm 9
Matthew 17:14–20

Sunday

AUGUST 8

By faith Abraham, when put to the test, offered up Isaac, and he who had received the promises was ready to offer his only son, of whom it was said, "Through Isaac descendants shall bear your name."

—HEBREWS 11:17–18

The test of your trust is this: can you relinquish even the very thing that seems absolutely essential for the fulfillment of God's promises to you?

Wisdom 18:6–9
Psalm 33
Hebrews 11:1–2, 8–19 or 11:1–2, 8–12
Luke 12:32–48

Monday

AUGUST 9

• SAINT TERESA BENEDICTA OF THE CROSS (EDITH STEIN), VIRGIN AND MARTYR •

Like the bow which appears in the clouds on a rainy day was the splendor that surrounded him. Such was the vision of the likeness of the glory of the LORD.

—EZEKIEL 1:28

There are things so breathtakingly lofty and beautiful that words can never do them justice. Knowing this, we summon up the best images we can—and leave it at that.

But, Lord, as we lift our hearts to contemplate these pale reflections of you, shine on us the radiance of your glory.

Ezekiel 1:2–5, 24–28
Psalm 148
Matthew 17:22–27

Tuesday

AUGUST 10

• SAINT LAWRENCE, DEACON AND MARTYR •

Whoever loves his life loses it, and whoever hates his life in this world will preserve it for eternal life.

—JOHN 12:25

"As much as we keep of ourselves, so much we lose of God," said Catherine of Siena, who was well-enough acquainted with the marketplace to recognize both a bad investment and a bargain when she saw one.

So which part of my life do I really want to keep?

2 Corinthians 9:6–10
Psalm 112
John 12:24–26

Wednesday

AUGUST 11

• SAINT CLARE, VIRGIN •

If your brother sins [against you], go and tell him his fault between you and him alone. If he listens to you, you have won over your brother.

—MATTHEW 18:15

Maybe because he came off as sly and shifty, Stan was one of the least popular kids at school. When Emily figured out that he was definitely the person who had stolen her headphones, it would have been satisfying to tell her friends and confirm their negative impressions of him. Instead, she confronted Stan privately and gave him a chance to make restitution. As she discovered, no one had ever related to Stan so straightforwardly.

Ezekiel 9:1–7; 10:18–22
Psalm 113
Matthew 18:15–20

Thursday

AUGUST 12

Son of man, you live in the midst of a rebellious house; they have eyes to see but do not see, and ears to hear but do not hear, for they are a rebellious house.

—EZEKIEL 12:2

In his first days on the management team, John felt uneasy about the company's unjust treatment of bottom-rung workers in other countries. Since everyone else seemed to view it as standard operating procedure, though, he quickly made his peace with it.

We who live in the "rebellious house" of societies whose trends are often at odds with God's ways need objective standards against which to measure our shifting values—stable, basic guides like, say, the church's social teaching and the Ten Commandments.

Ezekiel 12:1–12
Psalm 78
Matthew 18:21–19:1

Friday

AUGUST 13

• SAINT PONTIAN, POPE AND MARTYR • SAINT HIPPOLYTUS, PRIEST AND MARTYR •

God indeed is my savior;
I am confident and unafraid.
My strength and my courage is the LORD,
and he has been my savior.

—ISAIAH 12:2

If I thought more about my Savior's strength and less about my own weakness and deficiencies, I could truly live "confident and unafraid." Provided, of course, that I absolutely gave up on trying to save myself.

Ezekiel 16:1–5, 60, 63 or 16:59–63
Isaiah 12:2–6
Matthew 19:3–12

Saturday

AUGUST 14

• SAINT MAXIMILIAN MARY KOLBE, PRIEST AND MARTYR •

My sacrifice, God, is a broken spirit;
God, do not spurn a broken, humbled heart.
—PSALM 51:19

After his wife was killed by a drunk driver, Darrell took a time-out from praying. "I'm so angry and confused I don't dare present myself to God just yet," he confided to a friend. Then one day he gave up trying to make himself presentable and just threw himself before the Father in bitter anguish. That's when Darrell discovered that prayer comes in many forms, including the wordless presentation of a desolate, shattered heart.

Ezekiel 18:1–10, 13, 30–32
Psalm 51
Matthew 19:13–15

Sunday

AUGUST 15

• THE ASSUMPTION OF THE BLESSED VIRGIN MARY •

[A] princess arrayed in Ophir's gold
comes to stand at your right hand.
—PSALM 45:10

Until she was an adult, a cradle Catholic friend of mine thought that this feast was so named because the church makes the assumption that Mary was taken into heaven! Mary's body-and-soul entrance into eternal glory is not mere speculation, however. It's a solid reality that gives cause for great rejoicing: "Suddenly my soul was uplifted to behold and contemplate the Blessed Virgin Mary in glory. . . . I was filled with marvelous delight, and the sight did produce in me most immense joyfulness. The glorious Virgin was praying for the human race" (Blessed Angela of Foligno).

Vigil:
1 Chronicles 15:3–4, 15–16; 16:1–2
Psalm 132
1 Corinthians 15:54–57
Luke 11:27–28

Day:
Revelation 11:19; 12:1–6, 10
Psalm 45
1 Corinthians 15:20–27
Luke 1:39–56

Monday

AUGUST 16

• SAINT STEPHEN OF HUNGARY •

Now someone approached him and said, "Teacher, what good must I do to gain eternal life?" He answered him, . . . "If you wish to enter into life, keep the commandments." He asked him, "Which ones?" And Jesus replied, "'You shall not kill; you shall not commit adultery. . . .'" The young man said to him, "All of these I have observed. What do I still lack?"

—MATTHEW 19:16–20

Is this young man an eager beaver whose impetuous zeal outstrips his capacity for sacrifice? Is he a legalist who seeks to determine precisely which actions will guarantee the desired result? Is he a "fishing for compliments" type exhibiting a bit of smugness about his model life? Is he a sincere seeker? What do you think?

Ezekiel 24:15–24
Deuteronomy 32:18–21
Matthew 19:16–22

Tuesday

AUGUST 17

[I] feared that these foes would mistakenly boast,
"Our own hand won the victory;
the LORD had nothing to do with it."
For they are a people devoid of reason,
having no understanding.
—DEUTERONOMY 32:27–28

So quick to take credit for the good, to assign blame for the bad. So quick to indulge in a bit of flattering revisionist history, even as we recount our personal stories of God's interventions and the Spirit's leadings. So quick to magnify and present ourselves as truly spiritual and capable people—a real credit to God.

Forgive us, Lord. Have mercy!

Ezekiel 28:1–10
Deuteronomy 32:26–28, 30, 35–36
Matthew 19:23–30

Wednesday

AUGUST 18

• SAINT JANE FRANCES DE CHANTAL, RELIGIOUS •

[T]he owner of the vineyard said to his foreman, "Summon the laborers and give them their pay. . . ." When those who had started about five o'clock came, each received the usual daily wage. So when the first came, they thought that they would receive more, but each of them also got the usual wage. And on receiving it they grumbled against the landowner.

—MATTHEW 20:8–11

My nephew was perfectly satisfied with the little surprise toy he had been given—until his brother was given one too. Then he began to wail. "Why are you crying?" my sister asked him. "Just because he got something, it doesn't take anything away from what you have." The logic escaped my wailing nephew. Somehow, he felt diminished by his sibling's good fortune.

Unfortunately, I could relate to the way he felt.

Ezekiel 34:1–11
Psalm 23
Matthew 20:1–16

Thursday

AUGUST 19

• SAINT JOHN EUDES, PRIEST •

But when the king came in to meet the guests he saw a man there not dressed in a wedding garment. He said to him, "My friend, how is it that you came in here without a wedding garment?" But he was reduced to silence.

—MATTHEW 22:11–12

Think of how happy you are when you've had the foresight to have that "absolutely perfect" outfit dry-cleaned in advance of a party—and consider how blessed you'll be if you exercise similar foresight about what you'll be wearing for eternity.

Ezekiel 36:23–28
Psalm 51
Matthew 22:1–14

Friday

AUGUST 20

• SAINT BERNARD, ABBOT AND DOCTOR OF THE CHURCH •

Then you shall know that I am the LORD, when I open your graves and have you rise from them, O my people! I will put my spirit in you that you may live.

—EZEKIEL 37:13–14

You will bring us back to life, but not in an impersonal, coldly sterile, or standoffish way. No, with the closeness of a mouth-to-mouth resuscitation, you will breathe your Spirit into our deadness, and we will arise to a whole new way of living.

Ezekiel 37:1–14
Psalm 107
Matthew 22:34–40

Saturday AUGUST 21

• SAINT PIUS X, POPE •

Whoever exalts himself will be humbled; but whoever humbles himself will be exalted.

—MATTHEW 23:12

Once, I actually heard someone claim—without the slightest trace of irony—that a certain difficult experience "brought my humility to new heights."

How quickly pride infiltrates even our noble aspirations!

Ezekiel 43:1–7
Psalm 85
Matthew 23:1–12

Sunday

AUGUST 22

Endure your trials as "discipline."

—HEBREWS 12:7

As you struggle to pick up your cross today, consider this commonsense perspective from St. Augustine:

"Who would want troubles and difficulties? You command us to endure them, not to love them. No person loves what he endures, though he may love the act of enduring."

Isaiah 66:18–21
Psalm 117
Hebrews 12:5–7, 11–13
Luke 13:22–30

Monday
AUGUST 23

• SAINT ROSE OF LIMA, VIRGIN •

Woe to you, scribes and Pharisees, you hypocrites.

—MATTHEW 23:13

"It is not hypocritical if one's deeds fail to match one's words," St. Francis de Sales points out. "I no more believe I am perfect because I talk about perfection than I should believe myself Italian because I speak Italian."

But woe to us if we try to present ourselves to others as if there were no gap between our thoughts and deeds and our good intentions!

2 Thessalonians 1:1–5, 11–12
Psalm 96
Matthew 23:13–22

Tuesday

AUGUST 24

• SAINT BARTHOLOMEW, APOSTLE •

Philip found Nathanael and told him, "We have found the one about whom Moses wrote in the law, and also the prophets, Jesus son of Joseph, from Nazareth." But Nathanael said to him, "Can anything good come from Nazareth?" Philip said to him, "Come and see."

—JOHN 1:45–46

The invitation to "come and see" confronts us with the same decision that faced Nathanael: will we take the time to just hang out with Jesus? Unless we go to him and remain with him, how will we come to recognize the Son of God in this carpenter from ancient Galilee?

Revelation 21:9–14
Psalm 145
John 1:45–51

Wednesday

AUGUST 25

• SAINT LOUIS OF FRANCE • SAINT JOSEPH CALASANZ, PRIEST •

[W]e did not act in a disorderly way among you, nor did we eat food received free from anyone. On the contrary, in toil and drudgery, night and day we worked, so as not to burden any of you. . . . In fact, when we were with you, we instructed you that if anyone was unwilling to work, neither should that one eat.

—2 THESSALONIANS 3:7–8, 10

Am I invoking any pious excuses to exempt myself from my legitimate responsibilities? Do I indulge in idle speculations about my Christian faith that sidetrack me into futile occupations, inaction, and laziness? As I carry out my daily work, do I do it "from the heart, as for the Lord" (Colossians 3:23)?

2 Thessalonians 3:6–10, 16–18
Psalm 128
Matthew 23:27–32

Thursday

AUGUST 26

Be sure of this: if the master of the house had known the hour of night when the thief was coming, he would have stayed awake and not let his house be broken into. So too, you also must be prepared.

—MATTHEW 24:43–44

An ounce of prevention is worth a pound of cure. A stitch in time saves nine. Prevention is the best medicine. Or, as a Vermont proverb puts it, a clean cesspool means never having to pay for typhus serum.

1 Corinthians 1:1–9
Psalm 145
Matthew 24:42–51

Friday

AUGUST 27

• SAINT MONICA •

Then the kingdom of heaven will be like ten virgins who took their lamps and went out to meet the bridegroom. Five of them were foolish and five were wise. The foolish ones, when taking their lamps, brought no oil with them, but the wise brought flasks of oil with their lamps.

—MATTHEW 25:1–4

Unless we fuel our Christian life with basics like prayer and the sacraments, study, and good works, we'll run out of gas long before reaching our intended destination.

1 Corinthians 1:17–25
Psalm 33
Matthew 25:1–13

Saturday

AUGUST 28

• SAINT AUGUSTINE, BISHOP AND DOCTOR OF THE CHURCH •

From heaven the LORD looks down
and observes the whole human race. . . .
[T]he LORD's eyes are upon the reverent,
upon those who hope for his gracious help.
—PSALM 33:13, 18

My niece Jessie was nervous the first time she had to sing a solo a cappella. But sitting in the audience was her sister, Aimée, who flashed her a secret sign and an encouraging wink. Buoyed by that vote of confidence, Jessie turned in a stellar performance.

Lord, as you gaze down on me today, let me glance up and catch your look of encouragement. Give me the confidence I need to sing my little song in a way that brings you honor.

1 Corinthians 1:26–31
Psalm 33
Matthew 25:14–30

Sunday

AUGUST 29

[Y]ou have approached . . . Jesus, the mediator of a new covenant, and the sprinkled blood that speaks more eloquently than that of Abel.

—HEBREWS 12:22, 24

Cain's murderous act of violence left evidence that cried out for justice. "What have you done!" God said to him. "Listen: Your brother's blood cries out to me from the soil!" (Genesis 4:10).

The supreme act of violence that was the Crucifixion left evidence that cries out more loudly still. Incredibly, though, every drop of Jesus' blood is a plea for mercy.

Sirach 3:17–18, 20, 28–29
Psalm 68
Hebrews 12:18–19, 22–24
Luke 14:1, 7–14

Monday

AUGUST 30

He unrolled the scroll and found the passage where it was written:
"The Spirit of the Lord is upon me,
because he has anointed me
to bring glad tidings to the poor.
He has sent me to proclaim liberty to captives
and recovery of sight to the blind,
to let the oppressed go free."

—LUKE 4:17–18

Jesus, we feel both daunted and privileged that you call us to continue your mission on earth. May our words and actions announce your freedom and glad tidings to everyone around us. May we do all we can to help others know you as Healer and Savior.

1 Corinthians 2:1–5
Psalm 119
Luke 4:16–30

Tuesday

August 31

[N]o one knows what pertains to God except the Spirit of God. We have not received the spirit of the world but the Spirit that is from God, so that we may understand the things freely given us by God.

—1 CORINTHIANS 2:11–12

Nicky dug up every chrysanthemum bulb in the flower bed: he thought they were weeds. Damian mistook the salt for the sugar and ruined the apple pie. Luisa had no idea that the pieces of wood she used for kindling were parts of a dollhouse her husband was assembling.

Holy Spirit, help me to recognize the gifts you have given me, and show me how to use them. Unless you give me understanding, I'm liable to trash them by mistake.

1 Corinthians 2:10–16
Psalm 145
Luke 4:31–37

Wednesday

SEPTEMBER 1

For in God our hearts rejoice.

—PSALM 33:21

I celebrated when I heard that my cousin had pulled out of
her depression.
I exulted when our daughter found a good spouse.
I delighted in an unexpected visit with good friends I
hadn't seen in years.
I was grateful when the warranty covered the replacement
battery for our car.

But now tell me, Lord—
when was the last time my heart rejoiced not just
in your gifts,
but in *you*?

1 Corinthians 3:1–9
Psalm 33
Luke 4:38–44

Thursday

SEPTEMBER 2

When Simon Peter saw this, he fell at the knees of Jesus and said, "Depart from me, Lord, for I am a sinful man." For astonishment at the catch of fish they had made seized him. . . . Jesus said to Simon, "Do not be afraid; from now on you will be catching men."

—LUKE 5:8–10

Men? Is this supposed to be a comforting thought, Lord? Lately I haven't even been too good at what I know how to do—which is catch fish. How am I supposed to catch people? And what does that even mean? I don't get it. And yes, I *am* afraid. After all, I'm just an ordinary guy.

You know, Lord, sometimes you scare me.

1 Corinthians 3:18–23
Psalm 24
Luke 5:1–11

Friday

SEPTEMBER 3

• SAINT GREGORY THE GREAT, POPE AND DOCTOR OF THE CHURCH •

Commit your way to the LORD;
trust that God will act.
—PSALM 37:5

On June 24, 1959, an English doctor named Cicely Saunders was struck by this verse as she read her daily Scripture guide. She recognized it as a divine nudge and spent a day in the chapel praying for guidance about how to respond. Then she sat down and wrote up the proposal that would eventually launch the modern hospice movement, which has revolutionized end-of-life care and opened up the field of palliative medicine.

Teach us, Lord, to commit our paths to you and to leave the results in your hands.

1 Corinthians 4:1–5
Psalm 37
Luke 5:33–39

Saturday

SEPTEMBER 4

I am writing you this not to shame you, but to admonish you as my beloved children. Even if you should have countless guides to Christ, yet you do not have many fathers, for I became your father in Christ.

—1 CORINTHIANS 4:14–15

My father was a mild-mannered man, not naturally inclined to be confrontational. In raising his children, though, he did what he had to do. He steered us lovingly in the right direction, even when the process involved some unpleasantness. On this, his birthday, I pay tribute to him and to all who have played the role of "father in Christ" for me.

Who has played that role in your life?

1 Corinthians 4:6–15
Psalm 145
Luke 6:1–5

Sunday

SEPTEMBER 5

Teach us to count our days aright,
that we may gain wisdom of heart.
—PSALM 90:12

Maybe wisdom isn't so much about attempting to count the unknowable as it is about learning how to render a good account at the inevitable.

Wisdom 9:13–18
Psalm 90
Philemon 9–10, 12–17
Luke 14:25–33

Monday

SEPTEMBER 6

• LABOR DAY •

Your boasting is not appropriate. Do you not know that a little yeast leavens all the dough?

—1 CORINTHIANS 5:6

A news item reports on the ecological threat posed by Asian carp, an invasive species that gobbles up plankton and crowds out other fish as it migrates up the Mississippi. Some biologists call the carp "river rabbits" because they breed so quickly. More than fourteen hundred of them were found at a single site in a river where not one had been discovered the year before.

Carp, yeast, boasting—some things start small but go on to effect dramatic, rapid changes.

1 Corinthians 5:1–8
Psalm 5
Luke 6:6–11

Tuesday

SEPTEMBER 7

In those days he departed to the mountain to pray, and he spent the night in prayer to God. When day came, he called his disciples to himself, and from them he chose Twelve, whom he also named apostles.

—LUKE 6:12–13

Before narrowing down the field from seventy-two disciples (Luke 10:1) to twelve apostles, Jesus spent a whole night in prayer seeking the Father's will. How much more do we need to pray for guidance in our decisions big and small—we who are far less attuned to the Father's voice?

1 Corinthians 6:1–11
Psalm 149
Luke 6:12–19

Wednesday

SEPTEMBER 8

• THE NATIVITY OF THE BLESSED VIRGIN MARY •

We know that all things work for good for those who love God, who are called according to his purpose.

—ROMANS 8:28

For their wedding Mass, two friends of mine chose a song that featured this verse. In the thirty years since then, they have known some real ups and many deep downs—difficult job situations, unrelenting financial stress, problems with children, persistent serious illness.

Do they still think that "all things work for good"? Yes! And with conviction strengthened by experience, they belt it out even more loudly as the roller-coaster ride of their married life continues.

Micah 5:1–4 or Romans 8:28–30
Psalm 13
Matthew 1:1–16, 18–23 or 1:18–23

Thursday

SEPTEMBER 9

• SAINT PETER CLAVER, PRIEST •

But rather, love your enemies and do good to them, and lend expecting nothing back; then your reward will be great and you will be children of the Most High, for he himself is kind to the ungrateful and the wicked.

—LUKE 6:35

The milk of human kindness flows through my veins—until some crazy driver cuts me off . . . until I hear that arrogant politician expanding on his latest bad idea . . . until the telemarketer phones again as I'm about to bite into my sandwich . . .

How different I am from you, Father! I can't even wish good for the people who provide the daily opportunities for my little deaths to self. You even wish good for all who killed your Son. Please, help me be like you.

1 Corinthians 8:1–7, 11–13
Psalm 139
Luke 6:27–38

Friday
SEPTEMBER 10

To the weak I became weak, to win over the weak. I have become all things to all, to save at least some. All this I do for the sake of the gospel.

—1 CORINTHIANS 9:22–23

Todd was well-read and well-grounded in his faith, and he assumed that the other members of his parish Scripture study group were like him. But many of his comments confused them or went over their heads. Seeing this, Todd took a more helpful approach, training himself to listen carefully and to make his comments fewer, but also clearer.

Self-discipline isn't only about physical asceticism. It also means setting aside our own inclinations and conforming ourselves to others' needs in order that they may hear the gospel more clearly.

1 Corinthians 9:16–19, 22–27
Psalm 84
Luke 6:39–42

Saturday

SEPTEMBER 11

I will show you what someone is like who comes to me, listens to my words, and acts on them. That one is like a person building a house, who dug deeply and laid the foundation on rock; when the flood came, the river burst against that house but could not shake it because it had been well built.

—LUKE 6:47–48

As I write this, one year to the day after the unthinkable happened in New York and Washington and Pennsylvania, I can't help wondering what may have happened by the time you read it, on the third anniversary. One thing I know: in this uncertain world, only Jesus is rock solid. If we cling to the Living Word, we'll never be shaken—no matter what else may collapse around us.

1 Corinthians 10:14–22
Psalm 116
Luke 6:43–49

Sunday

SEPTEMBER 12

Or what woman having ten coins and losing one would not light a lamp and sweep the house, searching carefully until she finds it? And when she does find it, she calls together her friends and neighbors and says to them, "Rejoice with me because I have found the coin that I lost." In just the same way, I tell you, there will be rejoicing among the angels of God over one sinner who repents.

—LUKE 15:8–10

The woman finds the lost coin. Does God find the lost soul? Jesus' parable could sound as though the sinner returns through his own effort and initiative.

But isn't repentance itself the evidence that God is taking the initiative? How could we return to God unless he had searched us out and given us the grace to do it?

Exodus 32:7–11, 13–14
Psalm 51
1 Timothy 1:12–17
Luke 15:1–32 or 15:1–10

Monday

SEPTEMBER 13

• SAINT JOHN CHRYSOSTOM, BISHOP AND DOCTOR OF THE CHURCH •

In giving this instruction, I do not praise the fact that your meetings are doing more harm than good. First of all, I hear that when you meet as a church there are divisions among you, and to a degree I believe it.

—1 CORINTHIANS 11:17–18

The first rule of medicine should also be our basic ground rule for church assemblies and all of Christian living: First, do no harm.

1 Corinthians 11:17–26, 33
Psalm 40
Luke 7:1–10

Tuesday

SEPTEMBER 14

• THE EXALTATION OF THE HOLY CROSS •

[H]e humbled himself,
becoming obedient to death,
even death on a cross.
Because of this, God greatly exalted him
and bestowed on him the name
that is above every name.
—PHILIPPIANS 2:8–9

We adore you, O Christ, and we praise you,
for by your holy cross you have redeemed the world.
We bless and call upon your holy name,
which heals, strengthens, and saves us.

As we carry our cross, we who carry your name
offer you the sacrifice of our grateful, joyful hearts.

Numbers 21:4–9
Psalm 78
Philippians 2:6–11
John 3:13–17

Wednesday

SEPTEMBER 15

• OUR LADY OF SORROWS •

When Jesus saw his mother and the disciple there whom he loved, he said to his mother, "Woman, behold, your son." Then he said to the disciple, "Behold, your mother." And from that hour the disciple took her into his home.

—JOHN 19:26–27

Perfect obedience means persevering on the path God has called you to walk, even when it requires hurting those you love the most. Perfect love means being able to give someone else the joy of easing the pain that your perseverance has brought to those you love the most.

1 Corinthians 12:31–13:13
Psalm 33
John 19:25–27 or Luke 2:33–35

Thursday

SEPTEMBER 16

• SAINT CORNELIUS, POPE AND MARTYR • SAINT CYPRIAN, BISHOP AND MARTYR •

Now there was a sinful woman in the city who learned that he was at table in the house of the Pharisee. Bringing an alabaster flask of ointment, she stood behind him at his feet weeping and began to bathe his feet with her tears.

—LUKE 7:37–38

A bad-girl type barges into a men-only event in order to pay tribute to Jesus. Doesn't she care about what people will say? About coming off like a groupie? No, and no.

And what about us? Are we more concerned about public opinion than about finding our own ways to wash and anoint Jesus' feet? Does the gift of forgiveness ever move us to express our love with unashamed boldness? If not, we should sit at this woman's feet for a while.

1 Corinthians 15:1–11
Psalm 118
Luke 7:36–50

Friday

SEPTEMBER 17

• SAINT ROBERT BELLARMINE, BISHOP AND DOCTOR OF THE CHURCH •

[L]et me see your face;
when I awake, let me be filled with your presence.
—PSALM 17:15

Young Allan acted brave as he went in for corrective foot surgery, but he couldn't manage to look indifferent when he asked his mom, "Will you be here when I wake up?"

Lord, let me know your reassuring presence today. Awaken me to the ways in which I can see your face as I go about my daily routines.

1 Corinthians 15:12–20
Psalm 17
Luke 8:1–3

Saturday

SEPTEMBER 18

It is sown corruptible; it is raised incorruptible. It is sown dishonorable; it is raised glorious. It is sown weak; it is raised powerful. It is sown a natural body; it is raised a spiritual body.

—1 CORINTHIANS 15:42–44

You put a pasty mass of dough into the oven and it comes out a glorious golden loaf. You stick dry little grains into the ground and they bloom as colorful zinnias. You throw a capsule into a bowl of water and it swells up into a tiny sponge the shape of a cat. With so much experience of things that can have different forms of existence, how come we balk at the idea of physical resurrection?

1 Corinthians 15:35–37, 42–49
Psalm 56
Luke 8:4–15

Sunday

SEPTEMBER 19

First of all, then, I ask that supplications, prayers, petitions, and thanksgivings be offered for everyone, for kings and for all in authority, that we may lead a quiet and tranquil life in all devotion and dignity. This is good and pleasing to God our savior, who wills everyone to be saved and to come to knowledge of the truth.

—1 TIMOTHY 2:1–4

If I read the first sentence by itself, I'd be inclined to pray: "God, let everyone leave us alone so that we can go about our business and comfortably pursue our devotions."

But the second sentence tells me that "quiet and tranquil" describes a life with an evangelistic thrust. I'm challenged to pray for the kind of tranquillity that will help me step outside my cocoon and proclaim the gospel.

Amos 8:4–7
Psalm 113
1 Timothy 2:1–8
Luke 16:1–13 or 16:10–13

Monday

SEPTEMBER 20

• SAINTS ANDREW KIM TAEGON, PRIEST AND MARTYR, AND PAUL CHONG HASANG, MARTYR, AND THEIR COMPANIONS, MARTYRS •

Refuse no one the good on which he has a claim
when it is in your power to do it for him.
Say not to your neighbor, "Go, and come again,
tomorrow I will give," when you can give at once.
—PROVERBS 3:27–28

They never talked about the ways they annoyed each other, but their buried resentments made them adept at indirect communication. He expressed his disapproval by making her ask for every dollar she needed—even for groceries and the kids' school supplies. She paid him back by never being on time, by making him wait for her every chance she got. They didn't see it until they attended a married couples' retreat, but their control games were sabotaging their relationship.

Proverbs 3:27–34
Psalm 15
Luke 8:16–18

Tuesday

SEPTEMBER 21

• SAINT MATTHEW, APOSTLE AND EVANGELIST •

As Jesus passed on from there, he saw a man named Matthew sitting at the customs post. He said to him, "Follow me." And he got up and followed him.

—MATTHEW 9:9

We quite rightly admire the generosity of spirit that led Matthew to spring to his feet and follow after Jesus with never a backward glance. But do we also appreciate what it must have cost Peter and Andrew, James and John to keep following Jesus once they realized that they'd be living in community with one of the hated tax collectors?

Ephesians 4:1–7, 11–13
Psalm 19
Matthew 9:9–13

Wednesday

SEPTEMBER 22

And as for those who do not welcome you, when you leave that town, shake the dust from your feet in testimony against them.

—LUKE 9:5

Every night you help me to shake off the day's failures and discouragements. In your presence, I rid myself of all that contaminates and lessens my trust in you. Cleansed and refreshed, I can greet the next day with renewed hope and determination to follow in your footsteps.

Proverbs 30:5–9
Psalm 119
Luke 9:1–6

Thursday

SEPTEMBER 23

Vanity of vanities, says Qoheleth,
vanity of vanities! All things are vanity!
What profit has man from all the labor
which he toils at under the sun?
—ECCLESIASTES 1:2–3

Utterly futile! Completely absurd! Totally in vain! The way I sometimes feel about laundry and dusting is apparently the way the sage Qoheleth felt about *all* human activity. While his harsh conclusion needs to be reinterpreted in the light of the Resurrection, it should spur us to ask: What profit do we hope to get out of life? What are we really working for?

Ecclesiastes 1:2–11
Psalm 90
Luke 9:7–9

Friday

SEPTEMBER 24

LORD, what are mortals that you notice them;
human beings, that you take thought of them?
They are but a breath;
their days are like a passing shadow.

—PSALM 144:3–4

That you not only notice us but find us worth dying for—may we never tire of marveling and rejoicing at the mystery of it!

Ecclesiastes 3:1–11
Psalm 144
Luke 9:18–22

Saturday
SEPTEMBER 25

Remember your Creator in the days of your youth,
before the evil days come
And the years approach of which you will say,
I have no pleasure in them.
—ECCLESIASTES 12:1

Cultivate the discipline of prayer while you're in good health, advised Cardinal Joseph Bernardin. It's harder to pray when you're in physical pain.

Today, try turning to God as if it were your first, last, or only chance to do so.

Ecclesiastes 11:9–12:8
Psalm 90
Luke 9:43–45

Sunday

SEPTEMBER 26

There was a rich man who dressed in purple garments and fine linen and dined sumptuously each day. And lying at his door was a poor man named Lazarus, covered with sores.

—LUKE 16:19–20

"He lay there, sitting like a gold coin beside the road, but even more valuable," comments St. John Chrysostom, who goes on to expand on the shining faith and patience of the poor man at the gate.

If the rich man had picked up that gold coin, his net worth would have gone through the roof.

Amos 6:1, 4–7
Psalm 146
1 Timothy 6:11–16
Luke 16:19–31

Monday

SEPTEMBER 27

• SAINT VINCENT DE PAUL, PRIEST •

In all this Job did not sin, nor did he say anything disrespectful of God.

—JOB 1:22

Heard in a homily: When things go wrong, don't go wrong with them.

Job 1:6–22
Psalm 17
Luke 9:46–50

Tuesday

SEPTEMBER 28

• SAINT WENCESLAUS, MARTYR • SAINT LAWRENCE RUIZ AND HIS COMPANIONS, MARTYRS •

On the way they entered a Samaritan village to prepare for his reception there, but they would not welcome him because the destination of his journey was Jerusalem. When the disciples James and John saw this they asked, "Lord, do you want us to call down fire from heaven to consume them?" Jesus turned and rebuked them, and they journeyed to another village.

—LUKE 9:52–56

Those whose destination is the heavenly Jerusalem can expect the same hostility that Jesus encountered on his way to the earthly Jerusalem. His response sets the standard for our own.

Job 3:1–3, 11–17, 20–23
Psalm 88
Luke 9:51–56

Wednesday

SEPTEMBER 29

• SAINTS MICHAEL, GABRIEL, AND RAPHAEL, ARCHANGELS •

Then I heard a loud voice in heaven say:
"Now have salvation and power come,
and the kingdom of our God
and the authority of his Anointed.
For the accuser of our brothers is cast out,
who accuses them before our God day and night."
—REVELATION 12:10

Which is why, in the meantime, we can handle that accusing voice in the way C. S. Lewis suggested: "The next time the devil reminds you of your past, remind him of his future."

Daniel 7:9–10, 13–14 or Revelation 12:7–12
Psalm 138
John 1:47–51

Thursday

SEPTEMBER 30

• SAINT JEROME, PRIEST AND DOCTOR OF THE CHURCH •

Carry no money bag, no sack, no sandals; and greet no one along the way.

—LUKE 10:4

Although Jimmy and Caroline talked a lot about trusting God, they always seemed eager to acquire new things, move up the social ladder, and live at prestigious addresses. What their children learned about trust came not from their parents' minisermons but from observing how the family maid approached her demanding life.

Job 19:21–27
Psalm 27
Luke 10:1–12

Friday

OCTOBER 1

• SAINT THÉRÈSE OF THE CHILD JESUS, VIRGIN AND DOCTOR OF THE CHURCH •

Have you ever in your lifetime commanded the morning
and shown the dawn its place. . . .
Have you comprehended the breadth of the earth?
Tell me, if you know all:
Which is the way to the dwelling place of light,
and where is the abode of darkness?
—JOB 38:12, 18–19

Astronomers have discovered a black hole at the heart of the Milky Way galaxy. More than three million times the size of our sun, it is an estimated thirty thousand light-years from Earth (that's six trillion miles times thirty thousand).

God of the universe, you are greater than I can comprehend! I will trust you even when I don't understand your ways.

Job 38:1, 12–21; 40:3–5
Psalm 139
Luke 10:13–16

Saturday
OCTOBER 2

• THE GUARDIAN ANGELS •

See that you do not despise one of these little ones, for I say to you that their angels in heaven always look upon the face of my heavenly Father.

—MATTHEW 18:10

If we always treated one another as precious "little ones" worthy of being loved and cherished, the angels would rejoice—and maybe get a break from guard duty every now and then.

Job 42:1–3, 5–6, 12–17
Psalm 91
Matthew 18:1–5, 10

Sunday

OCTOBER 3

[B]ear your share of hardship for the gospel with the strength that comes from God. . . .
Take as your norm the sound words that you heard from me, in the faith and love that are in Christ Jesus. Guard this rich trust with the help of the holy Spirit that dwells within us.

—2 TIMOTHY 1:8, 13–14

Guarding this "rich trust"—our faith—is not a matter of keeping it hidden away from anything that might challenge or stretch it. In this case, guarding has to do with bearing hardship to advance the gospel. We safeguard this particular treasure not by stashing it in the bank but by using it.

Habakkuk 1:2–3; 2:2–4
Psalm 95
2 Timothy 1:6–8, 13–14
Luke 17:5–10

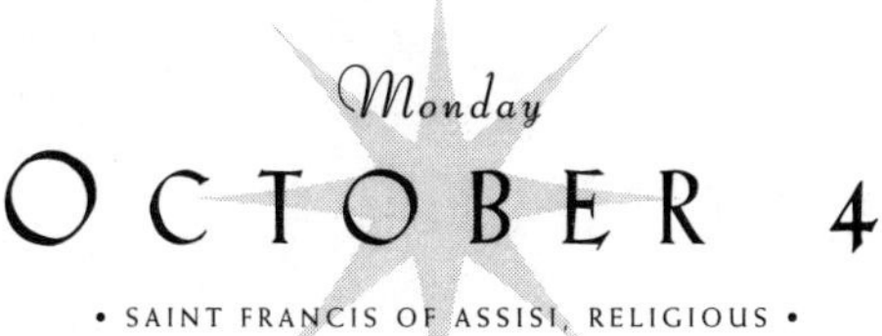

Monday OCTOBER 4

• SAINT FRANCIS OF ASSISI, RELIGIOUS •

Great are the works of the LORD,
to be treasured for all their delights.
—PSALM 111:2

The proliferation of inexpensive ethnic grocery stores in our city has turned my husband into an enthusiastic forager of unusual foods. Returning from a typical shopping expedition recently, he presented me with a jar of Persian whey, a can of spiny Malayan fruit called rambutan, and a Pakistani spice mix for cooking goat's head.

Even as I raise a quizzical eyebrow, Kevin's unabashed exulting at one tiny part of God's works reminds me to delight in everything the Lord has done.

Galatians 1:6–12
Psalm 111
Luke 10:25–37

Tuesday

OCTOBER 5

LORD, you have probed me, you know me:
you know when I sit and stand;
you understand my thoughts from afar.
—PSALM 139:1–2

You're like the service professionals who come to test for radon or get rid of bugs or combat the black mold in the bathroom. Come into my house, Lord, and show me what needs doing:

"Probe me, God, know my heart;
try me, know my concern.
See if my way is crooked,
then lead me in the ancient paths"
(Psalm 139:23–24).

Galatians 1:13–24
Psalm 139
Luke 10:38–42

Wednesday

OCTOBER 6

• SAINT BRUNO, PRIEST • BLESSED MARIE-ROSE DUROCHER, VIRGIN •

Then after fourteen years I again went up to Jerusalem. . . . I presented to them the gospel that I preach to the Gentiles—but privately to those of repute—so that I might not be running, or have run, in vain.

—GALATIANS 2:1–2

Every writer needs an editor. Every leader needs advisers who speak the truth without flattery. Every corporation needs honest stockholders to hold it accountable. Every traveler into a dangerous country needs a guide who knows the pitfalls.

Guidance, support, honest feedback, constructive criticism—who supplies (or might supply) these services for you?

Galatians 2:1–2, 7–14
Psalm 117
Luke 11:1–4

Thursday OCTOBER 7

• OUR LADY OF THE ROSARY •

What father among you would hand his son a snake when he asks for a fish? Or hand him a scorpion when he asks for an egg? If you then, who are wicked, know how to give good gifts to your children, how much more will the Father in heaven give the holy Spirit to those who ask him?

—LUKE 11:11–13

We have a Father who stands ready to give us an inexhaustible supply of the world's greatest gift. We have a Brother who died so that we could receive it. We have a mother who never stops telling us to open our hearts to our Father's and our Brother's generosity. Why do we hold back?

Our Lady of the Rosary, pray for us!

Galatians 3:1–5
Luke 1:69–75
Luke 11:5–13

Friday

OCTOBER 8

Scripture, which saw in advance that God would justify the Gentiles by faith, foretold the good news to Abraham, saying, "Through you shall all the nations be blessed."

—GALATIANS 3:8

I sit here contemplating the fact that my life has been deeply affected by an act of trust made by one man thousands of years ago . . . which leads to some sober reflecting about the ripple effect of my own actions and decisions for good or ill.

Galatians 3:7–14
Psalm 111
Luke 11:15–26

Saturday

OCTOBER 9

• SAINT DENIS, BISHOP AND MARTYR, AND HIS COMPANIONS, MARTYRS •
SAINT JOHN LEONARDI, PRIEST •

Rely on the mighty LORD;
constantly seek his face.
Recall the wondrous deeds he has done.
—PSALM 105:4–5

Lawrence loved to tell how God had led him out of a driven, workaholic lifestyle that was ruining his closest relationships. Somewhere along the line, though, he started introducing subtle details that put him in a better light and made him out to be nobly heroic. Once he'd gotten fuzzy about exactly who had worked the wondrous deed of his conversion, Lawrence's self-reliance emerged—but with a pious veneer.

A word to the wise: guard the memory!

Galatians 3:22–29
Psalm 105
Luke 11:27–28

Sunday

OCTOBER 10

As he was entering a village, ten lepers met [him]. They stood at a distance from him and raised their voice, saying, "Jesus, Master! Have pity on us!" And when he saw them, he said, "Go show yourselves to the priests." As they were going they were cleansed. And one of them, realizing he had been healed, returned, glorifying God in a loud voice; and he fell at the feet of Jesus and thanked him.

—LUKE 17:12–16

If that one had not returned to report that all ten lepers had been cleansed "as they were going," how would anyone have known what God had done for them?

If all my expressions of gratitude to God are private and not public, how will anyone know what God has done for me?

2 Kings 5:14–17
Psalm 98
2 Timothy 2:8–13
Luke 17:11–19

Monday

OCTOBER 11

• COLUMBUS DAY •

Blessed be the name of the LORD
both now and forever.
From the rising of the sun to its setting
let the name of the LORD be praised.
—PSALM 113:2–3

From east to west, from morning to evening, in our world of clocks and calendars and in the realms where time does not exist—may your holy name be always praised, hallowed, loved, thanked, remembered, declared, and desired!

Galatians 4:22–24, 26–27, 31–5:1
Psalm 113
Luke 11:29–32

Tuesday

OCTOBER 12

The Lord said to him, "Oh you Pharisees! Although you cleanse the outside of the cup and the dish, inside you are filled with plunder and evil. You fools! Did not the maker of the outside also make the inside? But as to what is within, give alms, and behold, everything will be clean for you."

—LUKE 11:39–41

Religious on the outside, selfish on the inside—is that me too?

If the answer is yes, I can repent and take note of the remedial penance Jesus recommends: offer practical, material help to people who are in need.

Galatians 5:1–6
Psalm 119
Luke 11:37–41

Wednesday

OCTOBER 13

[T]he fruit of the Spirit is love, joy, peace, patience, kindness, generosity, faithfulness, gentleness, self-control.

—GALATIANS 5:22–23

"You're different. Why?" my sister wanted to know.

"What do you mean?" I asked, all blushing innocence.

"You're more joyful, peaceful . . . " Jeanne didn't know it, but I had returned to the church. Though I hadn't been feeling "spiritual," she had noticed a change.

Years later, I can't say I detect much fruit of the Spirit on my branch of the vine. But leaving results to the Master Gardener, I try to receive all the sun and rain, fertilizer and insecticide that come my way.

Galatians 5:18–25
Psalm 1
Luke 11:42–46

Thursday

OCTOBER 14

• SAINT CALLISTUS I, POPE AND MARTYR •

Woe to you, scholars of the law! You have taken away the key of knowledge. You yourselves did not enter and you stopped those trying to enter.

—LUKE 11:52

A busy civic leader and philanthropist is shocked to discover that his assistant has been screening his mail so that appeals from certain worthy groups and individuals will never make it to his in box. "I was only trying to protect you," protests the biased assistant, who was really favoring the people in his old-boy network.

If you were the boss, what would you do?

Ephesians 1:1–10
Psalm 98
Luke 11:47–54

Friday

OCTOBER 15

• SAINT TERESA OF JESUS, VIRGIN AND DOCTOR OF THE CHURCH •

Meanwhile, so many people were crowding together that they were trampling one another underfoot.

—LUKE 12:1

Their motives weren't the best—they wanted to be fed or healed or to have their curiosity satisfied. And they weren't any less ruthless than those sharp-elbowed Italian grandmothers trying to get near the pope in St. Peter's Square. But you couldn't accuse these crowds of ignoring Jesus or treating him with indifference.

Can we say the same about ourselves?

Ephesians 1:11–14
Psalm 33
Luke 12:1–7

Saturday

OCTOBER 16

• SAINT HEDWIG, RELIGIOUS • SAINT MARGARET MARY ALACOQUE, VIRGIN •

[I] do not cease giving thanks for you, remembering you in my prayers, that the God of our Lord Jesus Christ, the Father of glory, may give you a spirit of wisdom and revelation resulting in knowledge of him.

—EPHESIANS 1:16–17

When my mother was five, she got her father to buy her a large statue of St. Anne. Now that statue of the patroness of grandmothers stands surrounded by photos of the twelve grandchildren who are faithfully and gratefully remembered in Mom's daily prayers.

What visual aids prompt and express your own prayers of intercession and thanks for the people you love?

Ephesians 1:15–23
Psalm 8
Luke 12:8–12

Sunday

OCTOBER 17

[P]roclaim the word; be persistent whether it is convenient or inconvenient; convince, reprimand, encourage through all patience and teaching.

—2 TIMOTHY 4:2

Before we seize on this directive as permission to trumpet the good news in any "in your face" manner that suits us, let's remember that it comes from a master evangelist who always tried to choose the approach that would be most winning for his audience.

Today, what would you do differently if you tried to adopt St. Paul's approach?

Exodus 17:8–13
Psalm 121
2 Timothy 3:14–4:2
Luke 18:1–8

Monday
OCTOBER 18

• SAINT LUKE, EVANGELIST •

All your works give you thanks, O LORD,
and your faithful bless you.
They speak of the glory of your reign
and tell of your great works.
—PSALM 145:10–11

Lately our dog has taken to installing himself in the prayer corner of our house for his morning nap, making himself small on the cushion in front of the icons. "Votive pup," my husband calls him.

Luke the evangelist praised God in a way that was appropriate for a human being with unique aptitudes and a Spirit-inspired calling. I like to think that Rupert the Shih Tzu praises God just by being the doggy self God created him to be.

2 Timothy 4:10–17
Psalm 145
Luke 10:1–9

Tuesday

OCTOBER 19

• SAINTS JOHN DE BRÉBEUF AND ISAAC JOGUES, PRIESTS AND MARTYRS, AND THEIR COMPANIONS, MARTYRS •

I will listen for the word of God.

—PSALM 85:9

And I will hear it when I still my heart and give God my full attention.

Ephesians 2:12–22
Psalm 85
Luke 12:35–38

Wednesday

OCTOBER 20

• SAINT PAUL OF THE CROSS, PRIEST •

You also must be prepared, for at an hour you do not expect, the Son of Man will come.

—LUKE 12:40

Be like the night nurse who watches attentively for the patients' call lights to go on. Be like the sales rep who never travels anywhere without her pager. Be like the employee who doesn't ever punch out until his boss has left the office. Be like the understudy who diligently rehearses her lines so that she can shine onstage if the leading lady gets sick.

Take it as your life motto: Be prepared.

Ephesians 3:2–12
Isaiah 12:2–6
Luke 12:39–48

Thursday

OCTOBER 21

For this reason I kneel before the Father, . . . that he may grant you in accord with the riches of his glory to be strengthened with power through his Spirit in the inner self, and that Christ may dwell in your hearts through faith; that you, rooted and grounded in love, may have strength to comprehend with all the holy ones what is the breadth and length and height and depth, and to know the love of Christ that surpasses knowledge, so that you may be filled with all the fullness of God.

—EPHESIANS 3:14, 16–19

There's a place for asking God to provide the occasional parking spot. But let's not lose sight of the big picture.

Ephesians 3:14–21
Psalm 33
Luke 12:49–53

Friday

OCTOBER 22

[L]ive in a manner worthy of the call you have received, with all humility and gentleness, with patience, bearing with one another through love, striving to preserve the unity of the spirit through the bond of peace.

—EPHESIANS 4:1–3

They each had a "right way" of doing things. He insisted that hot leftovers should go straight into the fridge; she thought they should cool off first. She said dusting should precede vacuuming; he thought the opposite. She used vegetable shortening in her piecrust; his mother had used lard. Somewhat amusing at first, the game degenerated into constant bickering.

The right way is the wrong way when it erodes love and respect.

Ephesians 4:1–6
Psalm 24
Luke 12:54–59

Saturday

OCTOBER 23

• SAINT JOHN OF CAPISTRANO, PRIEST •

[H]e said to the gardener, "For three years now I have come in search of fruit on this fig tree but have found none. [So] cut it down. Why should it exhaust the soil?" He said to him in reply, "Sir, leave it for this year also, and I shall cultivate the ground around it and fertilize it."

—LUKE 13:7–8

This tree has already enjoyed a grace period: Jewish law stipulated that the fruit of a fig tree was not to be picked for the first three years (Leviticus 19:23). But this tree has never produced a single fig! Even so, the owner agrees to another reprieve, and to an emergency measure (figs weren't usually fertilized).

Help, Lord—I'm like that fig tree! Help me to seize this time of grace and bear the fruits of repentance.

Ephesians 4:7–16
Psalm 122
Luke 13:1–9

Sunday

OCTOBER 24

For he is a God of justice,
who knows no favorites.
Though not unduly partial toward the weak,
yet he hears the cry of the oppressed.
—SIRACH 35:12–13

If we imagined ourselves as spectators in God's heavenly courtroom, what would we notice? Wouldn't we immediately be aware that the chamber was filled with the cries and prayers of the poor and oppressed?

Is this what we hear when we go to pray? Do we join in presenting the petitions of those who urgently need assistance and justice? Or are their voices always drowned out by our recitation of our own wants?

Sirach 35:12–14, 16–18
Psalm 34
2 Timothy 4:6–8, 16–18
Luke 18:9–14

Monday

OCTOBER 25

So be imitators of God, as beloved children, and live in love, as Christ loved us and handed himself over for us as a sacrificial offering to God for a fragrant aroma.

—EPHESIANS 5:1–2

Each life contributes its signature fragrance, filling God's house with an aroma infinitely more varied and wonderful than anything money can buy at our finest perfume counters.

Ephesians 4:32–5:8
Psalm 1
Luke 13:10–17

Tuesday

October 26

Again he said, "To what shall I compare the kingdom of God? It is like yeast that a woman took and mixed [in] with three measures of wheat flour until the whole batch of dough was leavened."

—Luke 13:20–21

He was the best of confessors, because he stepped back and allowed the Holy Spirit to lead the people who came to him. He offered guidance, but without imposing pet theories or a set approach. With his encouragement, people discovered their gifts and calling and became what God had created them to be.

Like some things in nature, some people have the genius and humility to function as barely perceptible agents for growth.

Ephesians 5:21–33 or 5:25–32
Psalm 128
Luke 13:18–21

Wednesday

OCTOBER 27

Strive to enter through the narrow gate.

—LUKE 13:24

The little girl I was babysitting wanted to be picked up and carried to bed. I was willing, but there was no way I could manage the load of dolls and books she wanted me to carry along with her!

Lord Jesus, please gather me in your arms and carry me through the narrow gate of salvation. I'm putting down all my toys and other encumbrances so that we can make it through.

Ephesians 6:1–9
Psalm 145
Luke 13:22–30

Thursday

OCTOBER 28

• SAINTS SIMON AND JUDE, APOSTLES •

The heavens declare the glory of God;
the sky proclaims its builder's craft.
One day to the next conveys that message;
one night to the next imparts that knowledge.
—PSALM 19:2–3

In nature's classroom, every day teaches the next about God's glory. As observers in that classroom, we should absorb the lesson and do all we can to hand on that same revelation from one generation to the next.

Ephesians 2:19–22
Psalm 19
Luke 6:12–16

Friday

OCTOBER 29

I am confident of this, that the one who began a good work in you will continue to complete it until the day of Christ Jesus.

—PHILIPPIANS 1:6

Rest assured that God is not like the foolish virgins who run out of oil before their master returns, or like the builder who begins a tower construction project that he can't complete for lack of funds.

Not only has the Lord counted the cost of saving and perfecting us—he has already paid the price.

Philippians 1:1–11

Psalm 111

Luke 14:1–6

Saturday

OCTOBER 30

When you are invited by someone to a wedding banquet, do not recline at table in the place of honor. . . . Rather, when you are invited, go and take the lowest place so that when the host comes to you he may say, "My friend, move up to a higher position."

—LUKE 14:8, 10

But bear in mind this helpful warning from St. Francis de Sales: "Let us never lower our eyes without humbling our hearts. Let us not make a show of wanting to be the last unless we really wish it."

Philippians 1:18–26
Psalm 42
Luke 14:1, 7–11

Sunday

OCTOBER 31

• HALLOWEEN • DAYLIGHT SAVING TIME ENDS •

But you have mercy on all, because you can do all things;
and you overlook the sins of men that they may repent.
For you love all things that are
and loathe nothing that you have made.

—WISDOM 11:23–24

Father, I am far from having your heart of mercy.
How often I sit in judgment of people!
How often I want to see "bad guys" come to a sudden bad end!
Help me to desire their salvation instead.
In the secret part of my heart, I do long to be merciful as you are merciful.
Today, help me to express this longing by remembering to pray especially for . . .

Wisdom 11:22–12:2
Psalm 145
2 Thessalonians 1:11–2:2
Luke 19:1–10

Monday

NOVEMBER 1

• ALL SAINTS •

After this I had a vision of a great multitude, which no one could count, from every nation, race, people, and tongue. They stood before the throne and before the Lamb, wearing white robes and holding palm branches in their hands.

—REVELATION 7:9

Grouchy? Look at St. Jerome. Anxious? So was St. Louise de Marillac. Ridiculously sensitive to criticism? St. Thérèse of Lisieux was like that too. Afraid of dying? St. Thomas More struggled with that very fear.

Just about every human foible was familiar to that victorious, white-robed multitude. So what's my excuse for not aiming for sanctity?

Revelation 7:2–4, 9–14
Psalm 24
1 John 3:1–3
Matthew 5:1–12

Tuesday

NOVEMBER 2

• THE COMMEMORATION OF ALL THE FAITHFUL DEPARTED (ALL SOULS) •
ELECTION DAY •

[T]he souls of the just are in the hand of God. . . .
Chastised a little, they shall be greatly blessed. . . .
As gold in the furnace, he proved them,
and as sacrificial offerings he took them to himself.
—WISDOM 3:1, 5–6

Yesterday's feast reminded us to ask for the great spiritual riches available to us through the intercession of the saints. Today's commemoration calls us to give generous spiritual assistance to other members of Christ's Body—our deceased brothers and sisters who are being purified.

Today is a good time to remember that the communion of saints is a communion of goods.

Wisdom 3:1–9
Psalm 27
Romans 5:5–11 or 6:3–9
John 6:37–40 or any readings taken from the Masses for the Dead, nos. 1011–1016

Wednesday

NOVEMBER 3

• SAINT MARTIN DE PORRES, RELIGIOUS •

[W]ork out your salvation with fear and trembling. For God is the one who, for his good purpose, works in you both to desire and to work.

—PHILIPPIANS 2:12–13

Infants who experience emotional deprivation develop a condition known as failure to thrive. So does our faith, if we neglect it.

God gives the growth, but we have to cooperate—which, in the spiritual life, is where the holy trio of prayer, fasting, and almsgiving enters in.

Philippians 2:12–18
Psalm 27
Luke 14:25–33

Thursday

NOVEMBER 4

• SAINT CHARLES BORROMEO, BISHOP •

[A]nd, upon his arrival home, he calls together his friends and neighbors and says to them, "Rejoice with me because I have found my lost sheep." . . . And when she does find it, she calls together her friends and neighbors and says to them, "Rejoice with me because I have found the coin that I lost."

—LUKE 15:6, 9

And the two celebrations will most likely involve two feasts whose costs exceed the value of the recovered sheep and coin! Lavish? Extravagant? Yes, says Jesus. That's how God is—always eager to rejoice and throw a party for every sinner who repents.

Philippians 3:3–8
Psalm 105
Luke 15:1–10

Friday

NOVEMBER 5

I rejoiced when they said to me,
"Let us go to the house of the LORD."
And now our feet are standing
within your gates, Jerusalem.
—PSALM 122:1–2

This is a pilgrim's psalm—a prayer said by someone who has traveled to Jerusalem and has just entered the city through one of its gates.

We can pray it as pilgrims too. We "go to the house of the Lord" whenever we step into a church to pray—and even when we turn to God in the quiet chapel of our hearts.

But do we have the same joyful eagerness to come into God's presence that this pilgrim psalmist has?

Philippians 3:17–4:1
Psalm 122
Luke 16:1–8

Saturday

NOVEMBER 6

The person who is trustworthy in very small matters is also trustworthy in great ones; and the person who is dishonest in very small matters is also dishonest in great ones. . . . If you are not trustworthy with what belongs to another, who will give you what is yours?

—LUKE 16:10, 12

Everything we have belongs to Another. The whole world is on loan! How can we prove our trustworthiness today?

Philippians 4:10–19
Psalm 112
Luke 16:9–15

Sunday

NOVEMBER 7

But the Lord is faithful; he will strengthen you and guard you from the evil one. We are confident of you in the Lord that what we instruct you, you [both] are doing and will continue to do.

—2 THESSALONIANS 3:3–4

When Paula was growing up, her parents let her know in many ways that they considered her a "bad seed." She lived up to their expectations.

When Paula got into trouble, her school counselor befriended her and let her know in many ways that she was capable of making a new start. His confidence was infectious and motivating. Over time, Paula lived up to the counselor's expectations too.

2 Maccabees 7:1–2, 9–14
Psalm 17
2 Thessalonians 2:16–3:5
Luke 20:27–38 or 20:27, 34–38

Monday

NOVEMBER 8

The earth is the LORD's and all it holds,
the world and those who live there.

—PSALM 24:1

Lying on my back on the cool grass, I look up into a pale blue sky crisscrossed with the chalky contrails of high-flying jets. Damascus, Dakar, Buenos Aires, Bangkok—far-off places brought so near, just a flight or an e-mail or an online newspaper away. The distance is in our heads.

Loving Lord of the world and its peoples, expand my vision and my heart. Help me be a responsible citizen of this world that I share with Syrians and Senegalese, Argentineans and Thais.

Titus 1:1–9
Psalm 24
Luke 17:1–6

Tuesday

NOVEMBER 9

• THE DEDICATION OF THE LATERAN BASILICA IN ROME •

[Y]ou are . . . God's building.

—1 CORINTHIANS 3:9

This edifice represents a cooperative effort between the Builder and the raw material, as the first-century bishop and martyr St. Ignatius of Antioch points out:

"Like stones of God's Temple, ready for a building of God the Father, you are being hoisted up by Jesus Christ, as with a crane (that's the cross!), while the rope you use is the Holy Spirit. Your faith is what lifts you up, while love is the way you ascend to God."

How will you advance this construction today?

Ezekiel 47:1–2, 8–9, 12
Psalm 84
1 Corinthians 3:9–11, 16–17
John 2:13–22 or any readings taken from the Common of the Dedication of a Church, nos. 701–706

Wednesday

NOVEMBER 10

• SAINT LEO THE GREAT, POPE AND DOCTOR OF THE CHURCH •

But when the kindness and generous love
of God our savior appeared,
not because of any righteous deeds we had done
but because of his mercy,
he saved us through the bath of rebirth
and renewal by the holy Spirit,
whom he richly poured out on us
through Jesus Christ our savior,
so that we might be justified by his grace
and become heirs in hope of eternal life.

—TITUS 3:4–7

My friend George Martin calls these verses "a magnificent summary of the gospel message." His suggestion: meditate on them by consciously including yourself among the "we," "our," and "us" references. Something to ponder today.

Titus 3:1–7
Psalm 23
Luke 17:11–19

Thursday

NOVEMBER 11

• SAINT MARTIN OF TOURS, BISHOP • VETERANS DAY •

Asked by the Pharisees when the kingdom of God would come, he said in reply, "The coming of the kingdom of God cannot be observed, and no one will announce, 'Look, here it is,' or, 'There it is.' For behold, the kingdom of God is among you."

—LUKE 17:20–21

In 1581, a Londoner named Henry Walpole attended the execution of Jesuit priest Edmund Campion. As the saint was being drawn and quartered, a drop of his blood splashed onto Walpole's coat. Suddenly converted, Walpole went on to become a Jesuit; he underwent the same bloody martyrdom thirteen years later.

Who can foretell when and where the kingdom of God will break forth? It is active, even where it is unacknowledged.

Philemon 7–20
Psalm 146
Luke 17:20–25

Friday

NOVEMBER 12

• SAINT JOSAPHAT, BISHOP AND MARTYR •

Look to yourselves that you do not lose what we worked for but may receive a full recompense. Anyone who is so "progressive" as not to remain in the teaching of the Christ does not have God; whoever remains in the teaching has the Father and the Son.

—2 JOHN 8–9

When we stop drawing on the deposit of faith, we're acting as foolishly as wannabe millionaires who sink their hard-earned savings into risky start-up companies that have no future.

2 John 4–9
Psalm 119
Luke 17:26–37

Saturday

NOVEMBER 13

• SAINT FRANCES XAVIER CABRINI, VIRGIN •

Happy are those who fear the LORD,
who greatly delight in God's commands.
—PSALM 112:1

"There are only two kinds of people," G. K. Chesterton wrote in his epigrammatic way—"those who accept dogmas and know it, and those who accept dogmas and don't know it."

If you want to be happy, choose your dogmas—and your teacher—carefully!

3 John 5–8
Psalm 112
Luke 18:1–8

Sunday

NOVEMBER 14

While some people were speaking about how the temple was adorned with costly stones and votive offerings, he said, "All that you see here— the days will come when there will not be left a stone upon another stone that will not be thrown down."

—LUKE 21:5–6

Massive stones from Herod's temple lie broken on the pavement where they fell, pushed over by Romans who destroyed the structure in A.D. 70. The sight inspires some soul-searching about the quality and future of smaller temples now under construction.

"Do you not know that you are the temple of God?" (1 Corinthians 3:16).

Malachi 3:19–20
Psalm 98
2 Thessalonians 3:7–12
Luke 21:5–19

Monday

NOVEMBER 15

• SAINT ALBERT THE GREAT, BISHOP AND DOCTOR OF THE CHURCH •

[W]hen he came near, Jesus asked him, "What do you want me to do for you?" He replied, "Lord, please let me see."

—LUKE 18:40–41

I was thirteen—and more nearsighted than I had realized—when I got my first glasses. It took me a while to adjust. Accustomed to viewing the world as an impressionist painting, I was unnerved by the sharp lines and clarity of things, by the way individual leaves stood out instead of merging into one large clump of green.

My sins and weaknesses unnerve me too. But how can I grow unless I'm willing to face the truth about myself, with whatever light and clarity God provides? Lord, give me the courage to say, "Please, let me see!"

Revelation 1:1–4; 2:1–5
Psalm 1
Luke 18:35–43

Tuesday

NOVEMBER 16

• SAINT MARGARET OF SCOTLAND • SAINT GERTRUDE, VIRGIN •

Behold, I stand at the door and knock. If anyone hears my voice and opens the door, [then] I will enter his house and dine with him, and he with me.

—REVELATION 3:20

Scholars point out that since the book of Revelation was written for Christians, Jesus' invitation did not originally refer to conversion but, quite likely, to the Eucharist.

Whether or not we feel worthy of inviting him under our roof, Jesus is on our doorstep, eager to share a meal that he has already provided.

Revelation 3:1–6, 14–22
Psalm 15
Luke 19:1–10

Wednesday

NOVEMBER 17

• SAINT ELIZABETH OF HUNGARY, RELIGIOUS •

Then the other servant came and said, "Sir, here is your gold coin; I kept it stored away in a handkerchief."

—LUKE 19:20

"You don't have to wear it," I told our daughter Anna. "It" was a loud and multicolored scarf I had knit her as a Christmas present—an investment of time and love, if not of skill. But every winter, Anna wraps that heavy scarf around her neck, and despite my apologetic remark, I won't say I'm not pleased she does.

Father, you give your children such good gifts. How pleased you must be when we use them instead of keeping them stored away.

Revelation 4:1–11
Psalm 150
Luke 19:11–28

Thursday

NOVEMBER 18

• THE DEDICATION OF THE BASILICAS OF SAINTS PETER AND PAUL, APOSTLES, IN ROME • SAINT ROSE-PHILIPPINE DUCHESNE, VIRGIN •

One of the elders said to me, "Do not weep. The lion of the tribe of Judah, the root of David, has triumphed, enabling him to open the scroll with its seven seals."
Then I saw standing in the midst of the throne and the four living creatures and the elders a Lamb that seemed to have been slain.

—REVELATION 5:5–6

O Lion of Judah, you are the Lamb of God!
Not by killing have you conquered, but by offering yourself as a sacrifice.
You are both all-powerful and all-merciful.
Your strength is the power of love,
your victory its triumph!

Revelation 5:1–10
Psalm 149
Luke 19:41–44
or (for the memorial of the dedication):
Acts 28:11–16, 30–31
Psalm 98
Matthew 14:22–33

Friday

NOVEMBER 19

Then Jesus entered the temple area and proceeded to drive out those who were selling things, saying to them, "It is written, 'My house shall be a house of prayer, but you have made it a den of thieves.'"

—LUKE 19:45–46

God doesn't take it lightly when people and things dedicated to his service are used as a legitimizing front for unholy goings-on. Neither should we.

Revelation 10:8–11
Psalm 119
Luke 19:45–48

Saturday

NOVEMBER 20

Blessed be the LORD, my rock,
who trains my hands for battle,
my fingers for war;
My safeguard and my fortress,
my stronghold, my deliverer.
—PSALM 144:1–2

There's a time for fighting temptation and a time for fleeing from it. Mercifully, the Lord has made provision for both tactics.

Revelation 11:4–12
Psalm 144
Luke 20:27–40

Sunday

NOVEMBER 21

• OUR LORD JESUS CHRIST THE KING •

Now one of the criminals hanging there reviled Jesus, saying, "Are you not the Messiah? Save yourself and us." The other, however, rebuking him, said in reply, "Have you no fear of God, for you are subject to the same condemnation? . . . [T]his man has done nothing criminal." Then he said, "Jesus, remember me when you come into your kingdom."

—LUKE 23:39–42

After a life of crime, the good thief gets into paradise—apparently without much of a stop in purgatory either—and is even traditionally remembered as St. Dismas. He got off easy? Maybe. On the other hand, how ready would you or I have been to put our confidence in Jesus at the very moment when he seemed most powerless?

It was, perhaps, heroic faith that led a dying thief to acclaim a dying King.

2 Samuel 5:1–3
Psalm 122
Colossians 1:12–20
Luke 23:35–43

Monday

NOVEMBER 22

• SAINT CECILIA, VIRGIN AND MARTYR •

Then I looked and there was the Lamb standing on Mount Zion, and with him a hundred and forty-four thousand who had his name and his Father's name written on their foreheads. I heard a sound from heaven like the sound of rushing water or a loud peal of thunder. The sound I heard was like that of harpists playing their harps.

—REVELATION 14:1–2

Counted as in a military census, the 144,000 followers of the Lamb stand marshaled behind their commander, ready to follow him into battle against evil. In their hands, they carry . . . harps.

An army of harpists?

Is that really so surprising? Haven't we all discovered that the enemy can be routed by our songs of praise to God?

Revelation 14:1–5
Psalm 24
Luke 21:1–4

Tuesday

NOVEMBER 23

• SAINT CLEMENT I, POPE AND MARTYR • SAINT COLUMBAN, ABBOT •
BLESSED MIGUEL AGUSTÍN PRO, PRIEST AND MARTYR •

Then let all the trees of the forest rejoice
before the LORD who comes,
who comes to govern the earth.
—PSALM 96:12–13

North American trees may not be doing much exulting right now. Norway maples and horse chestnuts are being decimated by the Asian long-horned beetle. A fungus threatens the Douglas fir. The Mediterranean fruit fly attacks citrus trees in Florida and California. During the last century, Asian fungi wiped out three and a half billion American chestnuts and forty million American elms.

In the new creation, though, all will be set right. When the Lord returns, trees—like human beings—will rejoice in him, disease-free.

Revelation 14:14–19
Psalm 96
Luke 21:5–11

Wednesday

NOVEMBER 24

• SAINT ANDREW DUNG-LAC, PRIEST AND MARTYR, AND HIS COMPANIONS, MARTYRS •

Just and true are your ways,
O king of the nations.
Who will not fear you, Lord,
or glorify your name?
For you alone are holy.
All the nations will come
and worship before you.
—REVELATION 15:3–4

This song of praise is a celebration of fruitful evangelization. Is this goal important to me? Do I cooperate in the church's work of helping people come to know and worship Jesus? Am I playing my part—through my example, words, material help and prayer support for missionaries around the world? How can I become more informed about Christian missionary efforts?

Revelation 15:1–4
Psalm 98
Luke 21:12–19

Thursday

NOVEMBER 25

• SAINT CATHERINE OF ALEXANDRIA, VIRGIN AND MARTYR •
THANKSGIVING DAY •

Enter the temple gates with praise,
its courts with thanksgiving.
Give thanks to God, bless his name;
good indeed is the LORD,
Whose love endures forever,
whose faithfulness lasts through every age.
—PSALM 100:4–5

Father, help me today not to give more attention to the turkey and the pumpkin pie than to you. Thank you for every good gift you have given me—most especially for the gift of adoption into your family.

Thanksgiving Day—proper Mass: In Thanksgiving (943–947), especially
Sirach 50:22–24
1 Corinthians 1:3–9
Luke 17:11–19

Revelation 18:1–2, 21–23; 19:1–3, 9
Psalm 100
Luke 21:20–28

Friday

NOVEMBER 26

I also saw the souls of those who had been beheaded for their witness to Jesus and for the word of God, and who had not worshiped the beast or its image nor had accepted its mark on their foreheads or hands. They came to life and they reigned with Christ.

—REVELATION 20:4

Originally, "worshiping the beast" probably referred to the practice of venerating the Roman emperor as divine. I don't know any Christians who have to worry about this today. On the other hand, I don't know any who don't have to fight the prideful, self-sufficient attitude that leads to glorifying a human being—that is, oneself—instead of God.

If we want to escape the mark of the beast, we have to wear the badge of humility.

Revelation 20:1–4, 11–21:2
Psalm 84
Luke 21:29–33

Saturday

NOVEMBER 27

Beware that your hearts do not become drowsy from carousing and drunkenness and the anxieties of daily life, and that day catch you by surprise like a trap. For that day will assault everyone who lives on the face of the earth. Be vigilant at all times and pray that you have the strength to escape the tribulations that are imminent and to stand before the Son of Man.

—LUKE 21:34–36

If I lived each day as if it were my last or my only one on earth, I would be better prepared to stand before the Son of man on the day of his return.

Revelation 22:1–7
Psalm 95
Luke 21:34–36

Sunday

NOVEMBER 28

• FIRST SUNDAY OF ADVENT •

They shall beat their swords into plowshares
and their spears into pruning hooks;
One nation shall not raise the sword against another,
nor shall they train for war again.
—ISAIAH 2:4

Is this going to be a mostly deck-the-halls Advent that leads into a feel-good, holly-jolly Christmas? Or are we going to give serious attention to the fact that we have yet to see the fulfillment of Christ's promise of peace?

In a world where even Christians take guns and swords to one another, our willingness to learn how to follow the Prince of Peace makes all the difference.

Isaiah 2:1–5
Psalm 122
Romans 13:11–14
Matthew 24:37–44

Monday

November 29

I say to you, many will come from the east and the west, and will recline with Abraham, Isaac, and Jacob at the banquet in the kingdom of heaven.

—MATTHEW 8:11

And, as Jesus indicates, many of those at table will be people we'd find it hard to even be in the same room with today! Wouldn't it make sense to ask the Host to widen our hearts so that they will be as inclusive as his guest list?

Isaiah 4:2–6
Psalm 122
Matthew 8:5–11

Tuesday

NOVEMBER 30

• SAINT ANDREW, APOSTLE •

As it is written, "How beautiful are the feet of those who bring [the] good news!"

—ROMANS 10:15

Like so many before me,
I fall at your feet, pierced for my sake.

With the penitent woman,
I anoint them with my tears and the ointment of my love.
With Mary of Bethany,
I sit at your feet and drink in your words.

I watch amazed as you lovingly wash my feet,
guide them into your path of peace,
and bid me bring your good news to others.

Romans 10:9–18
Psalm 19
Matthew 4:18–22

Wednesday

DECEMBER 1

Great crowds came to him, having with them the lame, the blind, the deformed, the mute, and many others. They placed them at his feet, and he cured them. The crowds were amazed when they saw the mute speaking, the deformed made whole, the lame walking, and the blind able to see, and they glorified the God of Israel.

—MATTHEW 15:30–31

After her best friend was killed, Kirsten fell into a deep, depressed silence. "What's the use of talking?" she told everyone who attempted to reach her. "It won't do any good." As they kept trying, though, she felt less alone.

Kirsten's reawakening to life and hope happened gradually. But to her friends and family, it was no less amazing than the instantaneous healings for which first-century crowds praised and glorified God.

Isaiah 25:6–10
Psalm 23
Matthew 15:29–37

Thursday

DECEMBER 2

I thank you for you answered me;
you have been my savior.
—PSALM 118:21

Thank you, God! Dave exulted inwardly as he closed the sale on his car. The car had a lot more problems than he had mentioned, but the buyer hadn't noticed.

Thank God I got to that cake before anybody else did, she thought, wiping crumbs off her lips.

Sometimes, our pious-sounding prayers of thanksgiving are nothing but perverse attempts to make God a party to our misdeeds and selfish desires. We thank God properly only when we know our need for a savior.

Isaiah 26:1–6
Psalm 118
Matthew 7:21, 24–27

Friday

DECEMBER 3

• SAINT FRANCIS XAVIER, PRIEST •

And out of gloom and darkness,
the eyes of the blind shall see.
—ISAIAH 29:18

One of my favorite CDs features a song in which the words of the well-known hymn "Amazing Grace" are set to the melody of the also well-known ballad about a "poor boy's" moral ruin, "House of the Rising Sun." It's a powerful interweaving, especially since the singers are black and the hymn was composed in the eighteenth century by a repentant slave trader. Even more evocative is that the elderly vocalists are fervent Christians who have been sightless all their lives. With every listening of their song, the Blind Boys of Alabama give me something to ponder.

Isaiah 29:17–24
Psalm 27
Matthew 9:27–31

Saturday

DECEMBER 4

• SAINT JOHN OF DAMASCUS, PRIEST AND DOCTOR OF THE CHURCH •

No longer will your Teacher hide himself,
but with your own eyes you shall see your Teacher,
While from behind, a voice shall sound in your ears:
"This is the way; walk in it,"
when you would turn to the right or to the left.
—ISAIAH 30:20–21

Online classes and distance-learning programs, language tapes and instructional videos—they all have their place. But if you want to learn discipleship, there's no substitute for a personal, live-in tutor. Fortunately, you can get the best if you're willing to learn and open to praying, "Come, Holy Spirit."

Isaiah 30:19–21, 23–26
Psalm 147
Matthew 9:35–10:1, 5–8

Sunday

DECEMBER 5

• SECOND SUNDAY OF ADVENT •

Then the wolf shall be a guest of the lamb,
and the leopard shall lie down with the kid.
—ISAIAH 11:6

At thirteen, Gary was an absolute beast who teased his sister without mercy or respite. Ten years later, he sent her a plane ticket and an invitation to visit for a week. With some trepidation, she accepted. Gary fixed her gourmet meals, bought her gifts, showed her the sights. Amazed, she returned home declaring that her brother had become "the nicest person in the whole world."

I have observed that when human beings seek God's kingdom, lambs can be the guests of wolves and come away delighted with the experience.

Isaiah 11:1–10
Psalm 72
Romans 15:4–9
Matthew 3:1–12

Monday

DECEMBER 6

• SAINT NICHOLAS, BISHOP •

And some men brought on a stretcher a man who was paralyzed; they were trying to bring him in and set [him] in his presence. But not finding a way to bring him in because of the crowd, they went up on the roof and lowered him on the stretcher through the tiles into the middle in front of Jesus.

—LUKE 5:18–19

If the door is locked, it looks for a window. If the phone is off the hook, it tries e-mail. If there are crowds at the gate, it scales the walls. Whatever the obstacles, love always finds a way.

Isaiah 35:1–10
Psalm 85
Luke 5:17–26

Tuesday

DECEMBER 7

• SAINT AMBROSE, BISHOP AND DOCTOR OF THE CHURCH •

Like a shepherd he feeds his flock;
in his arms he gathers the lambs,
Carrying them in his bosom,
and leading the ewes with care.
—ISAIAH 40:11

Mother Teresa told this story: "One day I discovered a poor child who would not eat. His mother was dead. I found a sister who looked very much like his mother. I told her to do nothing but take care of the child. His appetite returned."

Every sheep in the flock receives this kind of tailor-made, tender attention from the Great Shepherd—who expects that every sheep will then pass it along.

Isaiah 40:1–11
Psalm 96
Matthew 18:12–14

Wednesday

DECEMBER 8

• THE IMMACULATE CONCEPTION OF THE BLESSED VIRGIN MARY •

Where are you?

—GENESIS 3:9

After Adam disobeyed, God had to go searching for him in the Garden. That wasn't the case with a certain young woman from Nazareth. When the angel Gabriel came looking for her, she wasn't cringing behind a bush.

If your life is an open book before God, nothing stands in the way of your saying, "Here I am, Lord. I'm ready to do your will."

Genesis 3:9–15, 20
Psalm 98
Ephesians 1:3–6, 11–12
Luke 1:26–38

Thursday

DECEMBER 9

• SAINT JUAN DIEGO, HERMIT •

For I am the LORD, your God,
who grasp your right hand.
—ISAIAH 41:13

But if you're left-handed, he grasps your left. Whatever your need, however unique your situation, God finds a way to meet you in it.

Isaiah 41:13–20
Psalm 145
Matthew 11:11–15

Friday

DECEMBER 10

To what shall I compare this generation? It is like children who sit in marketplaces and call to one another, "We played the flute for you, but you did not dance, we sang a dirge but you did not mourn." For John came neither eating nor drinking, and they said, "He is possessed by a demon." The Son of Man came eating and drinking and they said, "Look, he is a glutton and a drunkard, a friend of tax collectors and sinners."

—MATTHEW 11:16–19

People who are hungry for the truth will receive it even from a messenger whose approach they find uncongenial. People who are indifferent or hostile to the truth will find a way to reject the message, whether or not they secretly admire the messenger.

Isaiah 48:17–19
Psalm 1
Matthew 11:16–19

Saturday

DECEMBER 11

• SAINT DAMASUS I, POPE •

Turn again, LORD of hosts;
look down from heaven and see;
Attend to this vine,
the shoot your right hand has planted.
—PSALM 80:15–16

The way the psalmist sees it, if he can only get God to look at the problem, it will be corrected: with God, seeing and doing are inseparable.

Wouldn't the world be a more just and peaceful place if our own seeing were more active? What if we paid attention to the needs of the person at the next desk? In the next house? On the next continent? And what if we followed up our taking notice by taking action?

Sirach 48:1–4, 9–11
Psalm 80
Matthew 17:9–13

Sunday

DECEMBER 12

• THIRD SUNDAY OF ADVENT •

Be patient, therefore, brothers, until the coming of the Lord. See how the farmer waits for the precious fruit of the earth, being patient with it until it receives the early and the late rains. You too must be patient.

—JAMES 5:7–8

See how the man looking to get in shape chooses regular exercise and healthy eating instead of the newest "quick weight-loss" fad diet . . . See how the budding novelist writes each day, turning out page after page of slowly improving prose . . . See how the yard-sale shopper keeps at it until she's found the vintage napkins to match her sister's tablecloth . . . See how the office assistant waits for just the right moment to ask for a raise.

You too must be patient.

Isaiah 35:1–6, 10
Psalm 146
James 5:7–10
Matthew 11:2–11

Monday

DECEMBER 13

• SAINT LUCY, VIRGIN AND MARTYR •

Good and upright is the LORD,
who shows sinners the way,
Guides the humble rightly,
and teaches the humble the way.
—PSALM 25:8–9

As she thought about it, Cindy felt deeply ashamed about having gotten the other kids to laugh at the new teacher and act up in class. After school let out, she stayed behind to offer an apology. It wasn't the easiest conversation Cindy had ever had, but she left feeling relieved and happy that she'd be able to go into the next day's class with a clean slate.

Numbers 24:2–7, 15–17
Psalm 25
Matthew 21:23–27

Tuesday

DECEMBER 14

• SAINT JOHN OF THE CROSS, PRIEST AND DOCTOR OF THE CHURCH •

A man had two sons. He came to the first and said, "Son, go out and work in the vineyard today." He said in reply, "I will not," but afterwards he changed his mind and went. The man came to the other son and gave the same order. He said in reply, "Yes, sir," but did not go.

—MATTHEW 21:28–30

I managed to report for work in your vineyard yesterday, Lord. But without your help, I won't get there today. Please give me the grace to renew my yes to you—and to repeat it more eagerly and wholeheartedly with every passing day.

Zephaniah 3:1–2, 9–13
Psalm 34
Matthew 21:28–32

Wednesday

DECEMBER 15

Love and truth will meet;
justice and peace will kiss.
Truth will spring from the earth;
justice will look down from heaven.
—PSALM 85:11–12

This psalm describes a harmony that will be perfectly realized only with the full coming of God's kingdom. Yet it is not a vague, ethereal image to store away until Jesus comes again. On the national level, it speaks about the sorts of issues that should preoccupy us all, from White House and Pentagon officials down to the newest voter.

No one is dispensed from the ongoing responsibility to help shape a government of justice and peace—not even in this postelection season.

Isaiah 45:6–8, 18, 21–25
Psalm 85
Luke 7:18–23

Thursday

DECEMBER 16

This is the one about whom scripture says:
"Behold, I am sending my messenger ahead of you,
he will prepare your way before you."
—LUKE 7:27

Over the course of your life, who have been the messengers sent to smooth your way to God? How have you received them? For whom is God calling you to perform the same service?

Isaiah 54:1–10
Psalm 30
Luke 7:24–30

Friday

DECEMBER 17

The book of the genealogy of Jesus Christ, the son of David, the son of Abraham.

—MATTHEW 1:1

When I visited Europe just after college graduation, I didn't trumpet my nationality. I just didn't want to be associated with the stereotype of the boorish American tourist.

The Son of God had no such reservations. Instead of springing into human history as an independent action hero, he readily assumed his place in a family with its share of skeletons in the closet. In relationship with all kinds of human beings—including the boorish—from the very beginning, Jesus is truly one of us.

Genesis 49:2, 8–10
Psalm 72
Matthew 1:1–17

Saturday

DECEMBER 18

For he rescues the poor when they cry out,
the oppressed who have no one to help.
He shows pity to the needy and the poor
and saves the lives of the poor.
—PSALM 72:12–13

As I write this, I know that today, more than 25,000 people around the world died from hunger and poverty. Nearly a sixth of Earth's population—840 million people—went to bed hungry.

How will my Christmas giving reflect this sober reality? How will I connect with God's rescue plan for the world's poor and needy?

Jeremiah 23:5–8
Psalm 72
Matthew 1:18–25

Sunday

DECEMBER 19

• FOURTH SUNDAY OF ADVENT •

"Behold, the virgin shall be with child and bear a son,
and they shall name him Emmanuel,"
which means "God is with us."
—MATTHEW 1:23

Jesus' birth announcement proclaims him as Emmanuel, "God with us." His last will and testament will be a commission to carry this good news to the world:

"Go, therefore, and make disciples of all nations, baptizing them in the name of the Father, and of the Son, and of the holy Spirit, teaching them to observe all that I have commanded you. And behold, I am with you always, until the end of the age" (Matthew 28:19–20).

Isaiah 7:10–14
Psalm 24
Romans 1:1–7
Matthew 1:18–24

Monday

DECEMBER 20

I will not ask!

—ISAIAH 7:12

"What do you want for Christmas?"

"Oh, nothing. Don't bother."

Let's not play this game with our Father! He has prepared the greatest gift imaginable for us, and it's ours for the asking. Let's not hold back. Let's ask!

Isaiah 7:10–14
Psalm 24
Luke 1:26–38

Tuesday

DECEMBER 21

• SAINT PETER CANISIUS, PRIEST AND DOCTOR OF THE CHURCH •

Let me see you,
let me hear your voice,
For your voice is sweet,
and you are lovely.
—SONG OF SONGS 2:14

You see beyond our unloveliness, and you call forth the hidden beauty we never knew we had. You teach us to view ourselves and others with your own eyes of love. You speak the sweet encouragement that draws us to you and to your ways. In you, Lord, we are made lovely.

Song of Songs 2:8–14 or Zephaniah 3:14–18
Psalm 33
Luke 1:39–45

Wednesday

DECEMBER 22

[M]y spirit rejoices in God my savior.

—LUKE 1:47

When your mind and heart are fixed on God, you can't help but rejoice, saints tell us. "The soul of one who loves God always swims in joy, always keeps holiday, and is always in a mood for singing," wrote St. John of the Cross. And according to St. John Chrysostom, even holy monks engaged in spiritual warfare "have no sadness. They wage war on the devil as though they were performing a dance"!

If you want the true "holiday spirit," seek the joy of loving God.

1 Samuel 1:24–28

1 Samuel 2:1, 4–8

Luke 1:46–56

Thursday

DECEMBER 23

• SAINT JOHN OF KANTY, PRIEST •

But who will endure the day of his coming?
And who can stand when he appears?
For he is like the refiner's fire,
or like the fuller's lye.
—MALACHI 3:2

Fullers work with cloth; they wash it, resize it, bleach it with a strong cleansing agent. Refiners work with metal; they melt solid gold and metal to a liquid from which dross can be removed. Jesus works with people: he purifies them and refashions them into new creations.

Which cleaning job do you think is the most difficult?

Which worker do you think is the most determined?

Malachi 3:1–4, 23–24
Psalm 25
Luke 1:57–66

Friday

DECEMBER 24

When King David was settled in his palace, and the LORD *had given him rest from his enemies on every side, he said to Nathan the prophet, "Here I am living in a house of cedar, while the ark of God dwells in a tent!"*

—2 SAMUEL 7:1–2

The first item on God's wish list isn't a magnificent cathedral. It's our unqualified consent to let ourselves become the temples of his Holy Spirit.

2 Samuel 7:1–5, 8–12, 14, 16
Psalm 89
Luke 1:67–79

Saturday

DECEMBER 25

• THE NATIVITY OF THE LORD • CHRISTMAS •

For today in the city of David a savior has been born for you who is Messiah and Lord. And this will be a sign for you: you will find an infant wrapped in swaddling clothes and lying in a manger.

—LUKE 2:11–12

In the stillness of an ordinary night, you snuck into our world as a helpless baby—and suddenly our ordinary lives were changed forever.

Christ child, we welcome you! We will make room for you in our lives and in our world.

Vigil:
Isaiah 62:1–5
Psalm 89
Acts 13:16–17, 22–25
Matthew 1:1–25 or 1:18–25

Dawn:
Isaiah 62:11–12
Psalm 97
Titus 3:4–7
Luke 2:15–20

Midnight:
Isaiah 9:1–6
Psalm 96
Titus 2:11–14
Luke 2:1–14

Day:
Isaiah 52:7–10
Psalm 98
Hebrews 1:1–6
John 1:1–18 or 1:1–5, 9–14

Sunday

DECEMBER 26

• THE HOLY FAMILY OF JESUS, MARY, AND JOSEPH •

My son, take care of your father when he is old;
grieve him not as long as he lives.
Even if his mind fail, be considerate with him;
revile him not in the fullness of your strength.
—SIRACH 3:12–13

Ever since he was a boy, it had been one of his favorite prayers: "Take, Lord, all my liberty. Receive my memory, my understanding . . . " But how much more fervently he prayed it when, in his mid-seventies, he became aware of his more than normal memory loss and realized where it would lead. It was the acid test of his surrender.

Sirach 3:2–7, 12–14
Psalm 128
Colossians 3:12–21 or 3:12–17
Matthew 2:13–15, 19–23

Monday

DECEMBER 27

• SAINT JOHN, APOSTLE AND EVANGELIST •

[T]he life was made visible;
we have seen it and testify to it
and proclaim to you the eternal life
that was with the Father and was made visible to us—
what we have seen and heard
we proclaim now to you,
so that you too may have fellowship with us;
for our fellowship is with the Father
and with his Son, Jesus Christ.
We are writing this so that our joy may be complete.

—1 JOHN 1:2–4

At Christmastime and all the time, the good news of Jesus' birth brings endless joy to both tellers and hearers. How will we share in that Nativity joy today? This week?

1 John 1:1–4
Psalm 97
John 20:1–8

Tuesday

DECEMBER 28

• THE HOLY INNOCENTS, MARTYRS •

When they had departed, behold, the angel of the Lord appeared to Joseph in a dream and said, "Rise, take the child and his mother, flee to Egypt, and stay there until I tell you. Herod is going to search for the child to destroy him."

—MATTHEW 2:13

One Herod searched for the child and failed to snuff out his life at its beginning. When that child became a man, another Herod helped bring about his death but failed to keep him in the tomb.

Everyone who makes room to welcome the Child should know that the Herods are still out for blood—and should stick very close to the manger and the cross.

1 John 1:5–2:2
Psalm 124
Matthew 2:13–18

Wednesday

DECEMBER 29

• SAINT THOMAS BECKET, BISHOP AND MARTYR •

Sing to the LORD, bless his name;
announce his salvation day after day.
Tell God's glory among the nations;
among all peoples, God's marvelous deeds.
—PSALM 96:2–3

If I limit myself to preaching by example and never proclaim God in my words, anyone who admires the way I live may jump to the conclusion that it's possible to live well without any help from God.

1 John 2:3–11
Psalm 96
Luke 2:22–35

Thursday

DECEMBER 30

When they had fulfilled all the prescriptions of the law of the Lord, they returned to Galilee, to their own town of Nazareth. The child grew and became strong, filled with wisdom; and the favor of God was upon him.

—LUKE 2:39–40

The tiny hands and feet, the fuzzy wisps of hair, the sweet smell of their precious newborn's head—the first-time parents marvel at it all. *Who is this child?* they wonder. *What will this tiny person be?* As the child develops, the mystery will unfold. Now comes the real adventure.

Lord, during the ordinary days of quiet growth that lie ahead, show us how to nurture what has come to birth in us.

1 John 2:12–17
Psalm 96
Luke 2:36–40

Friday

DECEMBER 31

• SAINT SYLVESTER I, POPE • NEW YEAR'S EVE •

[T]he light shines in the darkness,
and the darkness has not overcome it.
—JOHN 1:5

How have I experienced Jesus as the light of my life in this waning year? What darkness in my life needs his illuminating presence in the coming year? What darkness in the world do I especially want to bring to his attention?

Lord Jesus, you are my hope. I lift up my eyes to you.

You are the light of the world!

1 John 2:18–21
Psalm 96
John 1:1–18